Belief, Boldness, BIG Blessings

What People Are Saying

Belief, Boldness, BIG Blessings leaves a strong message of inspired vision, faith and perseverance as a divinely ordered path to success. The steps of faithful stewards are directed by the Lord. This book holds great promise of abundance in sales, as in moral and spiritual impact.

Dr. J A George Irish
The Right Honourable Professor

This collection of very inspirational stories invigorates your heart and soul and strengthens your belief. These stories exemplify the scripture James 2:17: "Thus also faith by itself, if it does not have works, is dead" (NKJV). It reminds us that we are born with greatness already in us, just waiting to be ignited by our faith and action. Our leap of faith will lead us to a lifetime of energy, growth, and blessings.

I recommend this book for all who are looking to move powerfully to the next stage of achievement in life.

John O. Jones
Minister, Empowerment Speaker,
Entrepreneur & Marriage Counselor

I have read and participated in several anthologies, but this one is a GAME CHANGER for sure. *Belief, Boldness, BIG Blessings* is an investment for your future. Your spirit will go "ahhh, just the confirmation, motivation and inspiration I needed." What makes this anthology delightfully different is that the testimonies are broken down in the areas of personal, business, education and identity. It is a towering achievement of testimonies that will transform your thoughts about life and its turns.

This book will stir your emotions and command you to do better. It will give you a panoramic scope of what it is to walk in faith. I personally know ten of the co-authors and was blown away by their transforming life chapters. Kudos to the visionary author, Ranelli Williams, for acting on obedience with this project. When you believe, take steps of boldness, your BIG blessing is waiting for you!

Donna Izzard (aka The "D.I.")
Author, Speaker, and Master Business Strategist

Belief, Boldness, BIG Blessings

The Faith Walker's Journey Expressed
Through 24 Powerful Testimonies

RANELLI WILLIAMS

purposely
created
PUBLISHING

BELIEF, BOLDNESS, BIG BLESSINGS

Published by Purposely Created Publishing Group™

Copyright © 2017 Ranelli Williams

All rights reserved.

Printed in the United States of America

ISBN: 978-1-947054-06-6

Dedication

I want to dedicate this book to the twenty-one individuals who said yes to this book project and followed through. Thank you for your transparency, which will undoubtedly positively inspire the lives of the people who read your stories. I celebrate you and your BIG Blessings as a result of your Belief and Boldness. God bless all your future endeavors.

Table of Contents

Section 1: Business Valiance
Six Faith Walkers Share Their Path to Success in Entrepreneurship

Section 4: Bold Rediscovery

Six Faith Walkers Share Their Journey to Peace and Fulfillment After Broken Relationships

Foreword

Cheryl Wood

Here is what I can promise...that after reading Belief, Boldness, BIG Blessings, you will feel more inspired than ever before to pursue your life's purpose with sheer tenacity. This beautifully written piece of work spearheaded by Ranelli Williams—a God-fearing woman, leader, and influencer—is a riveting compilation of personal stories of faith walkers who are committed to pursuing their God-given destiny even in the face of some of the most difficult challenges, losses, disappointments, and setbacks. Each of the twenty-four testimonials in this book serves as an integral reminder that we all have the ability to take our lives to the next level and avail ourselves of unlimited possibilities when we become bold enough to believe, take action, and develop a spirit of resilience.

The empowering testimonials in this book highlight the importance of building your dreams on a foundation of faith and belief, embracing mistakes and failures as a part of your process, taking one day at a time on your journey to greatness, and pressing through your own fears and doubts to ultimately take control of your destiny. For anyone who is yearning to live their life with greater passion, purpose, and intention, this book promises to feed your spirit and soul with much-needed confirmation that you have everything it takes to manifest the blessings you desire.

This amazing written work is a pivotal reminder that we each get to choose who we are becoming regardless of where we start and what we experience. By birthright, we are born for greatness, and we have every right to be a VICTOR amidst the trials and tribulations we experience along the way. God has created each of us with a unique gift that no one else can duplicate, and He is ready, willing, and able to open all the right doors for us to use those gifts to elevate our own lives and to help transform the lives of others.

As you allow the testimonials in *Belief, Boldness, BIG Blessings* to penetrate your heart, you will begin to experience the jolt needed to energize and equip you to create a shift in your life that puts you on a path to reaching your fullest potential. You will learn how to land on your feet even when all the odds seemed stacked against you. And you will reaffirm that you do not have to go into the battle to greatness all on your own. Rather, as so eloquently stated by Ranelli Williams, "God will go to battle with you."

I have read hundreds of books that aim to inspire, however, *Belief, Boldness, BIG Blessings* resonated with me on a deeper level as the contributing authors did not hold back from being transparent and vulnerable in sharing their raw, authentic truth.

As a mission-driven woman who has had to overcome my own challenges, fears, and roadblocks on my journey to success, I value the power of transparency demonstrated by Ranelli and the contributing authors in an effort to impact and transform the way other people think about their own ability to win big. As I continue to walk in my divine assignment of empowering women globally to boldly share their voice without shame or guilt, this book serves as a vital reminder to continue breaking outside of my comfort zone to grow to my next level and to keep speaking life into my own dreams. We can never receive too many reminders!

Belief, Boldness, BIG Blessings is truly a gift to every person who reads it. It is powerful and profound in teaching us that nothing can hold us back from achieving greatness except our own limited beliefs. I am confident that everyone who reads this book will develop an increased sense of urgency about pursuing their purpose and nurturing their possibilities without letup.

As you become inspired by the stories in this book, become bold and fearless in claiming what you want out of life, then audaciously go out and get it. Put the world on notice that your time to walk in greatness is now!

CHERYL WOOD

International Motivational Speaker
www.CherylEmpowers.com

Preface

In my first book, *Releasing the Fear & Walking in Faith*, I share biblical and practical tips and steps to conquering fear and courageously stepping out in faith. There's a freedom that comes with faith, prayer, meditation, and journaling, which is what's encouraged and demonstrated in that book. In this book, we take it a step further. We are celebrating the big blessings that are a result of exercising your beliefs and stepping out boldly.

The Bible says in John 14:12-14 ESV, "Truly, truly, I say to you, whoever believes in me will also do the works that I do; and greater works than these will he do, because I am going to the Father. Whatever you ask in my name, this I will do, that the Father may be glorified in the Son. If you ask me anything in my name, I will do it." When we believe, we ask, and Jesus said that when we ask anything in His name, He will do it. Do you understand that promise? All we have to do is believe and ask. It truly is that simple. As you read the remarkable stories of each coauthor in this book, just keep reminding yourself that if He (God) did it for them, He will do it for you as well. That's why He tells us in Matthew 7:7 NIV, "Ask, and it will be given to you; seek, and you will find; knock, and the door will be opened to you." God wants us to ask and He is waiting to grant us the desires of our hearts.

It is time we take our lives to the next level by allowing our passions and our purposes to meet. We are meant to prosper and make a difference in this world. It is our duty to leave a legacy for the next generation to follow. And guess what? We can. You can. So regardless of what's going on in your life, no matter how difficult life seems or how bombarded you are with the busyness, cares, and even chaos of this life, you can be, do, and have all that God has destined for your life. You can be free, you can be bold, you can make strides, you can accomplish your dreams, you can be successful, you can be prosperous, you can finish strong.

BUSINESS VALIANCE

*Six Faith Walkers Share Their Path to Success
in Entrepreneurship*

Trust and Believe and Watch God Show Up

Allison Arnett

Broke, busted, and disgusted. It sounds cliché, but that is exactly what I was when I decided to call out to God for more of Him. In March of 2015, I was on bed rest fighting pre-eclampsia two months before my third child was due for delivery. Three days after her birth at twenty-seven weeks, I was terminated from the job I had been working crazy overtime hours for during the previous few months. And get this—the company didn't even bother to tell me and refused to answer my calls and emails. I only found out because I asked the insurance company questions about my policy. Can you say "angry"? Because I was. Under that anger, though, I was hurt. I felt thrown away like trash—cast down. Have you ever felt discarded? If you have, then you know it doesn't feel good and you know exactly how I felt.

In between visits to my baby girl in the neonatal intensive care unit every day for six weeks, I had a lot of quiet time to think. I asked God why He would bless me with the highest paying job I had ever had, only to strip it away from me through no fault of my own. Why would He let me get to the mountaintop, show me the promise land, and then tell me it was not mine to possess? And God, what am I supposed to do now? I have rent, a new car note, and three mouths to feed.

I said, "God, how can I take control of my destiny?"

"Well," God said, "do you trust me?"

I said, "Of course, Lord."

He said, "You have over eighteen years of experience in accounting and you have over ten years of experience in graphic design. Let your gifts make room for you."

I said, "Okay," but I was terrified.

In retrospect, however, I can see God's hand at play. The Bible tells us, "Be ye angry, and sin not" (Ephesians 4:26 KJV). So many people egged me on and could not understand why I did not file a lawsuit against the company and possibly get enough money to take care of my family, but I did not feel led by God to do so. Instead, God used my anger as the fuel I needed to push me into full-time entrepreneurship. I had always had a heart to do it. Helping build others up and entrepreneurship were always things I did on the sideline, where it was safe. But like Harry Gray, the Arnold O. Beckman Professor of Chemistry at CalTech, said, "No one ever achieved greatness by playing it safe."

So I tucked in my doubt and fear, pulled up my big girl britches, and started on my way. I began watching instructional videos and live streams of other entrepreneurs, not only for ideas on how to take my passion from side hustle to business but also for hope and encouragement. In the process, God connected me with individuals to learn from, others to partner with, and some to befriend. I put the necessary items in place that I thought would make me look like a business: logo, website, Facebook business page, Twitter account, and Periscope account. I decided on a name, picked my colors, and cleaned up my personal Instagram account so I could use it for business instead.

I was spending countless hours learning and creating, but I still wasn't making any money. You know why? I was a silent-preneur. You know, the person who has a business you know nothing about because he or she doesn't tell anyone. My insecurities were robbing me. I had caused my fear and doubt to become thieves in my life. I was suffering from a case of "imposter syndrome." I did not feel qualified to serve others, and I kept thinking someone would discover I was a fraud. There was this constant feeling of "not enough" taunting me. "Who do you think you are?" it said. "You're an employee, not an entrepreneur." And to be quite honest with you, some days I believed it. Nonetheless, I continued on the journey to determine how to turn my passion into pretty pennies.

So let me tell you how good God is to me and about the time when I felt like I had something tangible to show for all my work toward this dream that only myself and handful of others believed in. Within twelve months of becoming a full-time entrepreneur, I had made five figures in my business. Five figures. I had never made anywhere close to that kind of money in one consecutive twelve-month span in all of my side hustle years. When I checked my bookkeeping records and realized my accomplishment, I almost could not believe it myself.

Can you imagine that feeling? Knowing that you've generated five figures in income doing what you love, working at your own pace, most of the time in your pajamas! Well let me attempt to describe the feeling for you. It's a feeling of pride, accomplishment, motivation, and assurance. Now don't get me wrong, I wasn't then, nor am I now, where I want or need to be financially. I still have major strides to take income-wise that will enable me to live comfortably and attain financial *and* time freedom. As a full-time entrepreneur with no formal investor, every dime I made in my business either went back into the business to pay expenses, to fund my trainings, or to pay my personal expenses. I still needed help, and I still needed to follow God's lead toward what He promised me.

Given a time machine, I would travel back to 2015 and affirm myself. I would first ask myself a few thought- and tear-provoking questions like: Who told you you're not enough? Aren't you receiving rave reviews for the results you're producing? Why won't you come out from behind the scenes and let yourself be seen? Do you or do you not believe that God will do just what He said He would do? Do you believe He will do it for you?

Then, after a warm and meaningful bear hug, I would look myself in the eyes and lovingly say, God has already equipped you with everything you need to accomplish that which He designed you for. You are enough. Not only are your supporters proud of and rallying for you, but so is God. You're doing great. There are people God has assigned to you that can't move forward with their visions until you move forward with yours. Come out from hiding so they can find you. God is not a man that He should lie, and He that began a good work in you shall complete it (Philippians 1:6). Take Him at His word. Before He formed you in your mother's womb, He knew you—intimately (Jeremiah 1:5). The real you. The you who He knew would make mistakes sometimes. He knew you. And He *still* called you to fulfill a specific purpose in His plan! So yes! God will do it for you too! You are an integral part of His divine plan for His kingdom. You matter to Him, and He will do it for you.

I would let myself know that clarity comes in the doing. I would tell myself to do it afraid and do it now, to not waste any more time wondering and wishing. Instead, charge ahead into the work and break down the barriers of time with effort. I would show myself how God keeps us by His might and power, how He supplies all our needs according to His riches and glory, and how He gives us the power to get wealth.

My 2015 self would be assured that just like the Lord promised her years ago, she is like a tree planted by the rivers of water, which bears her fruit in her season, and that everything she does will prosper (Psalm 1:3). I would implore her to let my words be her comfort and her cause to keep pushing when it seems our efforts are in vain. One thing I have learned in this life is that all things work together for good for those who love God and are called according to His purpose (Romans 8:28). If you find yourself in a similar situation and you are finding it difficult to see the bright side, I suggest you take a Romans 8:28 inventory check:

Do you love God?
Has He called you to do something?
Is there anything excluded from "ALL things"?
Are your troubles included in "ALL things"?
If you answered, yes, yes, no, yes, then guess what, this too is working together with everything else for your good. Perhaps you were brought to this moment for such a time as this. Perhaps

everything you've done to this point in your life was designed to bring you right where you stand; and X marks the spot.

You are exactly where you are meant to be and you got here right on time. Yes, even in your mistakes. God is not surprised by anything we do. I told you, before you were formed in your mother's womb, He knew you. So what's the message here? Trust and believe. If God placed you in existence, there is a purpose for your life. That purpose is not only going to bless you and others, but it is also ultimately to further His purpose and plans. What does this mean? If God gave you an assignment, then He is responsible enough and loving enough to give you the necessary tools and resources to accomplish that assignment. When we can trust God, we can step out on faith, follow God's lead, and take big risks to achieve big dreams; then we can see the promises of God fulfilled in our lives and the lives of those we are appointed and anointed to touch.

But it doesn't stop there. Belief is the cousin of Trust. You often will not see one without the other. *Merriam Webster Dictionary* defines trust as "belief that someone or something is reliable, good, honest, effective, etc.," and defines believe as "to accept something as true." So my question to you is, do you believe that you can trust God to do just what He says? Do you accept as true that God is reliable, good, honest, and effective, and He will show Himself as such in your life?

This whole entrepreneurship faith walk has been a test of my trust in God. It took me over twelve months and many conversations with God to understand the lesson that I am learning and that the portion of my life He is healing is all centered around trust. You see, my entire working career, I trusted myself and my abilities to be promoted based on my performance. God told me that He put me in my "rock bottom" position so that I could learn to trust in Him above all else.

During this journey, God has been with me every step of the way. He provides everything I need when I need it. Even in those moments when it looked like it was over and I would fail, God showed up and said, "I got you." He showed up in the form of divine connections with people who would push me and show me what He sees in me; financial blessings from unexpected sources; family and friends being there to take me in when I needed a helping hand; clients who would affirm the gifts He blessed me with; keeping a roof over my head, food in my belly, and my car in the driveway. Think back over your life. Can you see the places where God showed up for you? Those times when He said, "I got you"?

He said He would never leave us nor forsake us. I'm willing to bet that if you find yourself in a rock-bottom position right now that God is still with you. Ask God this question: "God, what am I learning here?" When you call Him, He will answer. Be open and receptive to the answer. Then I dare you to accept as truth that God is reliable, good, honest, and effective, and He will show Himself so in your life. I dare you to trust and believe.

"The only way God can show us He is in control is to put us in situations we cannot control." —Steven Furtick

It Was Already in My Hands

Delmar Johnson

Imagine returning home after a long stretch away to find yourself having to reacclimate to an environment that you had put in your rearview mirror for twelve years. Well, maybe not all the way in the rearview mirror because of family being there, but close enough. It was a year of transition; a year of figuring out where I belonged in the place where I was born and bred. Dare I say, it was even a culture shock: What do I do now? I returned home after losing everything—a client contract was cut short, my car was repossessed, and I was evicted. These situations can jar you a little and push you into a space where you must take the time to figure out some things in order to move forward.

It was me, God, and a whole lot of thoughts: What would or should be my next steps? What would those steps look like and which direction would be the best for me? I leaned back into what most would call the familiar, looking for a job and getting my mind back in position to forge through and survive. Can you relate to that? Trust me, as much as I had given thought to the hope of thriving, I had to tap back into survival mode so

I wouldn't go too far off course. You know, a place where your mind can reserve itself from going too far to the left or right.

So that's where this journey begins with me, as I chose to take one day at a time. A journey that was on the way to an idea, a vision if you will, that to this day continues to grow. But before getting to that point, there are some basics to get back to first. I did what most thinking, educated woman would do: get a job. As a woman who tapped into a part of herself that was never known to be there, the entrepreneur, the backup job seeker kicked in. Remember, I was in survival mode, so I did what I needed to do. A job was the immediate solution. Trying to find myself, coupled with the responsibility of caring for the one who gave me life, added a pressure that I did not know how to handle.

Let me ask you—have you ever faced something that you couldn't see how you were going to handle it, or if you could at all? Well, that's surely what happened to me and it smacked me right across my cheek. I didn't voluntarily sign up for it, but nevertheless, it seemed as though it was an appointment for the assignment at hand. This is where you have to say to yourself, God will not put on you more than you can bear, whether you believe it or not.

Now let's fast forward some. I jumped back into the job scene with both feet, albeit through temporary opportunities, and through one of those temporary assignments, I was led by God himself right into a vision I never saw coming. Who else could it have come from? It just had to be a God thing. That's how I chose to see it because it happened as though it had been waiting on me, all enveloped in a simple conversation, which is captured below.

First, allow me to preface that I was working as a recruiter hiring supervisors and associate staff. One day, one of the supervisors I had recruited and guided through the hiring process struck up a conversation while we both were leaving for the day. He seemed to be so fascinated by what I did for the company as a recruiter, vetting qualified candidates for the operations team, and through these simple words, I instantly received what I call a *divine download*: "You really should do that for other people and businesses who need that kind of help but don't really know how to do it."

Yes, it was as simple as that. I could barely contain my excitement. Have you ever had an idea that took over every space in your head and spirit because you didn't want to miss a thing, even if you didn't have a pen and paper to write it down as soon as you could? By the time I reached my car, I already had a name for my "whatever it was." In that moment, HR Brain for Hire first entered my psyche, and what that could look like flooded my senses. Not only how I could pull it off, but what I would offer, how I would get the word out, and what I needed to have in place to make it work. There was so much in my head at one time on the drive home; I couldn't wait to write it all down to see what it looked like on paper.

God's word says, "Write the vision, and make *it* plain upon tables, that he may run that readeth it" (Habakkuk 2:2 KJV). In writing the vision, it became clear, and I boldly acted on it. Never could I have fathomed the journey it would take me on. I didn't have a thirty-page business plan, nor were all the pieces in place before starting. That's one thing so many entrepreneurs get caught up in or make the mistake of thinking: every piece must be in place before starting. It's really in the starting that the pieces begin to fall into place so you can begin building the know, like, and trust factor. You further move through a process of weeding out what isn't working, how to attract your first clients or twentieth client, and how to wear all the hats that make a business sustainable. It was exhilarating yet scary not knowing how it would all turn out.

Over the course of the past six years, while working in my business, there have been many times I've been in a mental space where I wanted to hang it up and simply walk away. At one point, I did that very thing. That part of the journey no one ever really warned me about or prepared me for didn't seem worth it. I caught myself in the "comparison" game. Allow me to encourage you right here to never fall for the comparison game. It truly becomes a killer of your own dreams and visions for how you see yourself. The quicker you are clear about your "why" and your abilities to make things happen, the more prepared you are to mentally and emotionally move forward to see your ideas, dreams, and visions come true and become a part of your own solution, while also being the solution to others.

One thing's for sure: the divine downloads push you into action and you learn that working that "entrepreneurial venture" will be some of the hardest work you've ever done. I've been pushed, stretched, and brought to the very edge of seeing the vision for my business unfold little by little, day by day. Every time I wanted to throw in the towel, the fire in my belly wouldn't let me. The voice in my head wouldn't let me. The dream wouldn't let me.

Today, I continue to push myself and work toward an end goal. It's said so often that you must see the end goal and then work backwards to accomplish it. Sometimes that's easier said than done, so it's important for you to be still and listen to the voice in your spirit about your next step. Meditation and prayer will be very important for you as you take action toward your dreams and visions. Above all else, I believe if your mindset is focused on higher thoughts, you are elevated not only as a person but as the brand you are building. The mind truly is where everything begins. So it's vital to your well-being and the well-being of your idea and brand that your mind is in sync with the direction you are headed.

I have no regrets about the good and bad that I have encountered birthing and nurturing HR Brain for Hire. It has served as therapy for me while serving other entrepreneurs in creating structures and foundations for their brands to grow through building teams and systems. I thrive off serving and developing solutions for the small business community, which is a vital entity for the growth of the economy, through the creation of jobs, systems, and generation of revenue streams.

Truly, I can't even imagine where I would be mentally, emotionally, or even financially if this opportunity had not been presented to me through the channel of "surviving." God never ceases to amaze me in how he operates and extends us the opportunity to tap into what's already in us. He conveys to us in His word that we must use what's in our hands. He gives us the power to get wealth. Wealth not only to establish generational legacy within our families, but wealth that we have options and can invest in the kingdom.

I find taking daily and continuous actions toward fulfilling the divine downloads as my contribution not only to build up God's people in the marketplace, but also to build up who I am as a person and a contributing member in society. Seeking at all times a way to improve and stretch toward excellence is fuel that I choose to keep in the forefront of my mind. I ask you, what fuels you to build day by day, what you see and feel within yourself?

There are so many everyday distractions in the world that can so easily pull us away from the very thing we see or say we want. One thing to keep in mind is that not everyone will always be for what you do, or agree with what or how you do it. Always keep in the forefront of your mind that the vision, the idea, was not given to them; it was given to you. You have the responsibility to see it through, to accept and embrace the accountability and the burden of carrying that vision. Not a burden that is not worth carrying, but because it is a weight that you will have to seek balance in carrying.

The beauty of going inside yourself, inside your mind, and pulling out what others have not seen from your perspective, something that offers the very solution that others seek, is so gratifying. People won't always get what you do the first or second time around, but it is the power of you continuing to talk about it and execute your plans to make an impact upon those who are meant to be served by you.

There is the old saying that when the student is ready, the teacher appears. That's how I look at it. The more I speak on the importance of human resources solutions for the small business community, the more I talk about and educate those entrepreneurs about the necessity of HR. It becomes the best avenue to show that what HR Brain for Hire offers is viable and valuable to the growth and sustainability within the small business community.

From one client to the next, word of mouth spreads and helps to display your level of expertise and credibility. There is a saying in business that will never change: people do business with those they know, like, and trust. You cannot sit on the sideline and expect your audience to know you; you must get on the field and let them know what solutions you can offer them to make their life easier. Isn't that what it's all about? Remember this: it's not only important for you to position yourself as the "expert" in your lane; it's just as important as building relationships because it will be the fuel you will always need to see yourself growing and making a greater impact.

My hope in sharing my story is that you will be encouraged to tap into what you have in your hands. That you will get focused on that dream and cultivate it. Even more importantly, that you become more sensitive to what God has for your life. God wants us to be prosperous in all areas of our life. He wants to give us the desires of our hearts, which God himself has deposited. Your dreams have always been there; they are waiting on you to catch up through the actions you take toward them.

Health: Your Biggest Investment

Cherylann Jordan

My health journey began in 1978, the year I became a born-again Christian. In November of that year, my maternal grandmother, Amelia, was hospitalized with complications from diabetes and high blood pressure. She weighed over 300 pounds. After two weeks in the hospital, she died at age fifty-four.

As a new Christian, and with the concern of my grandmother's sudden passing, I delved into the Bible to learn all that I could about a healthier lifestyle. I discovered so many things about diet and food that I had never learned before. For example, I learned that God allowed men to use the meat for food after the flood due to the vegetation being destroyed by the flood. Before the flood, man lived up to 969 years very frequently; people born after the flood only lived some 400 or 500 years or so. The oldest recorded for that generation is 529 years. As years progressed, the life expectancy fell to only 120 years. God did that because of sin so that man could not live long enough to perpetuate evil. God finally reduced man's life expectancy to about seventy years. Psalm 90:10 NIV tells us, "Our days may come to seventy years, or eighty, if our strength endures."

I decided that if I only had seventy years, I wouldn't allow my stomach to be a graveyard for the flesh of those animals. I became a lacto-ovo-vegetarian for thirty years, from 1978 to 2008. In the midst of my health journey, in 2003, it seemed like history was repeating itself when my mother, Yvonne, died from health issues similar to my grandmother's. My mother suffered from high blood pressure and had to undergo her fifth hernia surgery. Within two weeks of having the surgery, she died. I made a commitment that that was not going to be my story. I wanted to leave a different legacy for my children and help as many people as possible do the same.

My big move happened in two phases. First, I gave up eating beef and pork after learning about how they affect the body. In the second phase, I gave up all flesh foods, including poultry and fish. For the most part, it was not a big deal because, in fact, my large family of nine—my two parents and their seven children—were so poor that we only ate meat on the weekends. By the time I had immigrated to the United States at the age of eighteen, I had never eaten a beef burger or hot dog.

In 1994, I started a health and wellness direct sales business. I did this in conjunction with my career as a civil engineer. In 2001, I retired from my civil engineer job to become a stay-at-home mom because I believed that my kids needed me at home more than anything else. I was able to then dedicate a little more time to health and wellness since I was no longer commuting to employment in New York City from Pennsylvania. I continued my home business selling wellness products and attended an online college to study to become a naturopath. As a stay-at-home mom, I saved myself $1,200 in daycare and commuting costs, and I was also able to focus on the two passions in my life: my children and health.

In 2008, I was at an impasse in my life. During that time, I had numerous struggles with my relationship with God. I considered relocating back to New York and I lost my grounding in many of my fundamental beliefs, including my diet. I did not pray as much as I should have or follow the principles of health that I know is God's plan. As a naturopathic doctor (ND) and wellness coach, I should have known better. I lost my mind and started eating chicken again for about eighteen months. I feel I must have lost my mind because eating meat was against everything that I had believed and practiced for thirty years! For much of that time, meat was not even allowed in my home. But then, for the first time in thirty years, my husband began cooking meat at home for our non-vegetarian children. The aroma of the cooking meat enthralled me, and over time, I began to eat chicken again. Not only did I enjoy eating chicken, but I forgot about what caused me to stop eating it in the first place. I started secretly eating the chicken my husband prepared for our children. When I finally told my kids, they were so shocked. My oldest daughter's jaw dropped—her mom was eating meat.

After those eighteen months, I started suffering from an extreme inflammation of the lips, which the doctors called cheilitis. No matter what we did, my lips would not heal. This is when I made a huge discovery: when you have a disease in one part of your body, it can spread to all parts of your body. The inflammation moved to my legs. If I would get a scrape or cut, my skin would grow to a large, deep, painful, itchy wound that would not heal. I didn't know what it was until my doctor did a biopsy and told me that it was the same inflammation from my lips but called lichen planus. This is a common disease that is inflammatory in nature. It affects the skin and the oral cavity, causing lesions of the mouth and skin.

Based on my extensive knowledge of health and wellness, I created my wellness program for inflammation. I prayed and searched my manuals from the Trinity School of Natural Health, where I was studying to obtain my doctorate of naturopathy, for an answer to the chronic inflammation, and God gave me the answer. He said, "What? Know ye not that your body is the temple of the Holy Ghost *which is* in you, which ye have of God, and ye are not your own?"

As an ND, I learned that it takes 120 days to replace new blood cells and about 45 days to impact change in the body, so I decided to go on a detox and juice journey in the fall of 2012. After about forty-five days, the blessing came and my lips began to heal. After trial and error, and suffering from constipation, I decided to change from juice extraction to whole food juicing. I continued to do this for seventy-five days. I ate raw foods like nuts, seeds, fruits, and vegetables. The results were amazing. My skin cleared up, and my lips became luscious, like the lips of a brand new baby.

That became another light bulb moment. I had seen my grandmother die from health-related issues when I was eighteen years old, and many years later, I saw my mom suffer the same fate. I realized then that this was a tragic pattern, and I wanted to do something about it. I was motivated by a desire to help other women not suffer the same experience, and I completed my ND degree in order to obtain as much knowledge as possible to help other people. I made a choice that that was not going to be my story. I wanted to have a healthy family and to live to see my children and grandchildren grow up. I do not want them to experience unnecessary health issues. By setting an example for my family, I am rewriting history for years to come and leaving a legacy of health and wellness. Future generations will not have to endure the same death sentence as my mother and grandmother.

In 2015, after seeing the results from following God's health plan and knowing my passion for health and wellness, I decided to accelerate that passion further. I made the bold move to switch from just being a marketer of health products to becoming a wellness coach full time. I became a practitioner for health and wellness to concentrate on assisting women to become healthy. One of the reasons I focus on women is because they feed their husbands and children and impact the entire family. I created the Rejuvenate Your Life Program with the goal to teach women, and more specifically women over forty, how to have better health now and to pass that knowledge on to their children and their grandchildren.

Your health is a major financial decision, and the reason I say that is because either you invest in prevention or you invest in getting well after you've gotten sick. The prevention investment is so much cheaper than the investment it takes to get well once you are sick. When you get sick, you can't work, earn money, function, operate your business, and most importantly, you can't be there for your children. You need a healthy body to be able to operate and do what God has called us to do. "Beloved, I wish above all things that thou mayest prosper and be in health, even as thy soul prospereth" (3 John 1:2 KJV). Whatever it is, this will be a financial decision that you have to make. The choice to be made is either before or after.

My desire for you is that you learn the secret to better health. You are awesome and incredible, and your best years are ahead of you as you move from your forties and into your fifties and sixties. I want you to have that vibrant health that you deserve. I pray that as you trust God, allow this chapter of this book to be the one thing that helps make your big, bold move to your fantastic health.

Walk in Your Freedom and Shine

Nataushia Miller

What do you want to be when you grow up?
"I want to be an artist and a writer," was my primary response as a child. However, I never had a clear vision of what my career would entail as an adult. Although some adults would say there's no money in any of that, all I knew was that money would not be an issue and I would get paid for doing what I loved! And as a child, I loved to write and draw.

What career will you pursue after college?
"I want to establish a youth program to help young people make a healthy transition from childhood to adulthood," was my response as a high school student. I understood there was no money in the human service industry, yet in my heart, I knew that money would not be an issue and I would get paid to do what I loved! And as a young adult, I loved helping others be and become their best.

As a college graduate struggling to obtain a good paying job, I battled frustration. I often questioned the Spirit of the Lord: How can I create the lifestyle my heart desires as an employee?

Which entrepreneurial endeavor aligns with the core of who I am and what I love to do? How do I become a lender and not a borrower? Little did I know that such answers would unfold through my faithfulness to fulfilling one little divine revelation: *The Idea.*

THE IDEA

"Your testimony as a Hurricane Katrina survivor and Dillard University college graduate is truly inspiring. We should talk to the First Lady to see if you could speak to our Heart to Heart Ministry at the cotillion ball," a woman from my church said. The two of us served as mentors of young teenage girls. At the end of every year, the ministry hosted a ball to celebrate the accomplishments of the young ladies.

I responded, "No, thank you. I'm not comfortable with sharing my story like that."

But in my mind, I thought I was unqualified. All I could think about was a few of my colleagues who possessed more powerful testimonies than me, and I began to wonder how I could get them to the ball without having to spend a lot of money since they were living in different states. I pondered over this for days until one night while driving home, I received *The Idea,* a divine revelation from the Lord: "Have your colleagues write a one-page testimony and create a beautiful testimonial portfolio for the girls."

That night, I arrived home in excitement and on a mission to make this portfolio collection a reality. I emailed my colleagues a statement request with the requirements and a deadline. Eleven of my colleagues responded by submitting their written piece.

By the time of the cotillion ball, I had over thirty testimonial portfolios, entitled *Relationship and Religion to Know the Difference*, ready to present to each of the young ladies at the ball! This accomplishment occurred in the fall of 2007, and I was oblivious that *The Idea* would later become *The Vision*.

THE VISION

In the fall of 2010, my heart's desires from childhood were continuing to evolve. I was married, completing my final year of a community leadership graduate program, working as a case manager for a nonprofit serving disadvantaged youth, interning for a nonprofit that specialized in community organizing, and expecting my first child, when I was interrupted by the Spirit of the Lord: "It's time to turn the testimonial portfolio into a book."

Immediately, I went to work. I developed a clear vision, mission, and purpose for the book as well as a timeline and a business plan. Then I emailed all my colleagues who had participated in the portfolio the complete book project packet with a letter requesting their contribution. Upon receiving all responses, I began researching the publishing process.

Not once did I think that my ignorance of the industry would keep me from making *The Vision* happen. However, although each of us thought we possessed a testimony for the second portion of the book (the first part is our original statements and the second our narratives), life happened. It was as if the commitment to the project unleashed Pandora's box. We all began to go through the tests, trials, and fiery darts of life simultaneously. Originally, we were to complete *The Vision* within two years, but the uncertainties and *The Test* of life turned those two years into ten.

THE TEST

I believe the most challenging times in life come not only to test our character but to reveal and release our authenticity. Two months after graduating from the American Baptist Seminary of the West with a master in community leadership, and two days before my first child was born in July 2011, my husband lost his job. Although he found new employment by October, he wasn't making nearly as much as before, and my little part-time position became an expense rather than additional income due to the commute. By January 2012, we had been evicted and were homeless for ten months that year while pregnant with baby number two, who was born December 2012.

That time was painful, however, in retrospect, it was the most pivotal turning point for me and my husband's lives—a blessing in disguise. It was *The Test* that shifted our mindsets from those of employees to those of entrepreneurs. We came to the realization that it is unwise to rely on one or two streams of income as an employee *only* and that if we wanted to take control of our financial destiny, we had to get creative to develop several streams of income as business owners.

Nevertheless, during *The Test*, I never lost sight of *The Vision*. My colleagues and I would have prayer calls and corporate fasting about the book project. I met and developed relationships with other entrepreneurs, speakers, authors of book compilations, and influential leaders who were doing what they loved while getting paid. I began to invest in myself by enrolling in their coaching and training programs, which supplied me with the knowledge, step-by-step processes, and resources that increased my capacity as a visionary. Such like-minded relationships and investments in my plan helped me cultivate strategy.

What began as twelve of us with the completion of *The Idea*, and nine of us with a commitment to *The Vision*, became four of us at the time of completion—*The Harvest*.

THE HARVEST

"We have to get you to come out and do a writer's workshop for our team," said my network marketing leader during our group training.

At the time of this training with my team, in the summer of 2015, I was two months away from releasing my first book, *Is FREEDOM your Reflection in the Mirror? Eight Steps to Overcoming Trauma*, and was in the last publishing stages for the ten-year book project that began as *The Idea*.

While driving home that night, I heard the Spirit of the Lord speak: "If you conduct a writer's workshop, you will not do it for free because you're going to launch your publishing company." That was the first time that I did not take immediate action; rather I just responded with one word: "Okay."

As we neared the completion of the book project, I considered publishing with the company founded by my business coach. Shortly after receiving the quote to move forward with her publishing services, the Spirit of the Lord spoke: "Don't be lazy. Publish the book yourself with your own publishing company."

After I completed a telecourse entitled *Create Your Own Book Compilation*, which my business coach presented, she said, "Now you have the tools, Nataushia, to publish the compilation you've been working on with your colleagues. You don't need my business to do it."

I spoke with my husband about it, and he was in total agreement with the Spirit of the Lord. "Let's do it!" he exclaimed.

So I began to ponder the thought of establishing a publishing company. What would we name it and why?

You see, initially, before receiving *The Idea,* I was seeking a way to create a platform for the testimonies of my colleagues to shine. *The Idea, The Vision, The Test*, and *The Harvest*, which was on the horizon, were never about me. They were about the lives of others. Then I remembered one of my favorite classes, an elective course, in high school. We would create the props for plays, control the sound and the lights, open and close the curtains, and run everything that happened behind the scenes of our theater performances and events. I loved creating the atmosphere for others to shine on stage. The elective course I grew to love was called Stagecraft.

In May 2016, I walked into *The Harvest*. With our publishing company, Stagecraft Publishing Inc., my husband and I published our ten-year book compilation project, *S.A.L.T. Sisters Accelerating Lives Together. Your Story Will Shine* became our company slogan. And what I love most about such an accomplishment is that we didn't stop there. We kept seeking, listening, obeying; we kept growing and going.

THE COMMISSION

Never underestimate the power of an idea! It is like the faith of a mustard seed. When you act to make an idea a reality, in turn, you give the Lord something to increase. Act courageously! When you receive a vision from the Lord, don't think about it—*do it*. Sometimes, you must act first before you can write the plan strategically and make it understandable. Sometimes, the action is *The Test*.

Never give up! No matter the storms of life you may encounter, do not lose focus of *The Vision*. Continue to water the concept with all that you can give, even if it is prayer alone due to life challenges. Keep growing and going! Get comfortable with being uncomfortable and when you find yourself comfortable, challenge yourself to go beyond your comfort zone. In other words, do not become complacent or content with one level of personal freedom, knowledge, or accomplishment. Stay actively engaged in your human development process by continuously striving for something fresh, original, and relevant. These are a few of the necessary ingredients for taking bold steps in your life that will produce significant blessings.

As for my personal journey, it was *The Test* component of my process that connected the dots of my now reality and my future destiny to my childhood desires and dreams—a lifestyle of freedom. I am no longer frustrated and can now see my desire for living life without money being an issue and getting paid to do what I love in the process of becoming a reality, *The Harvest*.

Therefore, I end my chapter with one of my poems:

I Don't Grind. I SHINE.

The term "grind" and legitimate entrepreneurship just don't

go hand in hand to me.

Last I checked, as a CEO of a company,

I do not reduce anything to fine particles by pounding or

crushing; rather I give forth, shed, and cast light.

I glisten, sparkle, and shine brightly, even at night.

I am not one to be on my "grind":

Hustling, working hard not smart, unfulfilled, tired, or hasty

as if I am running out of time or racing to be first in line.

Rather, I SHINE.

I take my time,

Knowing that success is who I am and not something I must

strive to obtain or acclaim because my Savior knows me by

name.

I SHINE.

My Savior instructed me to lift Him up, and He will draw indi-

viduals unto Himself.

It is why I placed that "grind" mentality on a thrown-out shelf.

I SHINE.

In obedience and humility before the Lord, knowing that He

will promote me in His time.

Bottom line, I don't need to "grind"

Because all things are possible when I step back and allow the

God in me to SHINE!

Why "grind" when you can SHINE?

Now go. *Walk in your freedom and shine!*

Get Out of Your Head and Say It

Veronica Ray

You are not yet where you are going, but no one expected you to be this far. Going the distance can be a treacherous journey. You have heard people say the road can get rough. I am Veronica Ray, owner and founder of Jigsaw & Associates, and I would like to affirm the entrepreneurial experience certainly has its ups and downs.

While my mother was certain to make sure I know who God is, I credit my learning or knowing of God at such an early age to my uncle, James, and granny. I would spend every Saturday night with my wonderful Uncle James, his wife, and his three daughters, so I could ride to church with them to hear my uncle preach. When I wasn't with my uncle, I was alongside my granny working in the nursing home, listening to her encourage residents, and often the workers too, with her Bible teachings. Developing a relationship with God and reading His word alongside my granny developed in me the importance of faith. Keeping your faith in God and understanding tough times are the necessary constructs to continuously increase your faith, promote essential growth, and provide learning opportunities that will cultivate a life one can only imagine.

Similar to how you establish a foundation in other areas of your life, it is also crucial that you build your empire on a solid foundation. It is my belief and experience that relying on the one greater than yourself will navigate you into your purpose and allow you to fulfill the desires of your heart. Execute your authority to call on God and ask Him for your needs, wants, and desires. One of my favorite scriptures is Psalms 37:4-6 NIV: "Take delight in the Lord, and He will give you the desires of your heart. Commit your way to the LORD; trust in Him and He will do this: He will make your righteous reward shine like the dawn, your vindication like the noonday sun."

Consider with me for a moment how layers of concrete are poured, one layer on top of the other, each layer providing stability for the next. Until eventually you have a road, sidewalk, or driveway. Even with each strategically poured layer, in a short few months, you will often find a few bumps and grooves that were not a part of the original foundation. Your foundation is much like the concrete. Although there will be bumps and grooves along the way, you too will persevere because a solid foundation—your belief in God—is what you stand upon.

Can you recall the day you awakened with the idea? You knew you were destined to build an empire and leave a legacy for your family. The idea was likely not an easy one to settle with. Many sleepless nights, wrestling with the endless thoughts running circles in your mind. You could see it, but you just weren't sure how. Former tax consultant turned entrepreneur, Mike Dooley, calls these thoughts "the cursed hows." I am here to tell you that when you follow God and ask Him the questions you need answers to, knock on His door when you are exhausted from working tirelessly to make it happen, and seek Him first before seeking others, He will make your path clear.

In this twenty-first century, marketing and advertising platforms are not the same. Less than ten years ago, communicating with your client via text message was regarded as unprofessional. Working from anywhere other than a brick-and-mortar location meant that you could not be trusted. Yet today, these are all acceptable and, in most cases, preferred methods of conducting business. So if you previously spent several years in corporate America, you might be having a difficult time eliminating your old beliefs and adjusting to this new way of doing business. If so, take this book to your car, write down a list of all the things you need help with and at least five things you are grateful for, and begin to speak aloud the things you have written.

Often, we have silent, pleading prayers. I am encouraging you to have a vocal, praising prayer with God today. Thank Him for bringing you this far, even if you are still thinking about the dream. Ask Him what your next step is. Tell Him what you want and ask Him to show you the way to it. Ask Him what the most suitable way to conduct your business is. Discuss your list with Him.

I started my business, Jigsaw & Associates, with a dream and a prayer. The first three months of business, my filing cabinet was a plastic tote, my main office was the dining room table, and my second office was in my car. I drove countless miles from one client to the next to provide accounting, payroll, tax, and business coaching services. From time to time, a client would request to meet in my office, so I would schedule meetings at an office complex with shared office space. This complex would eventually become the official corporate address for Jigsaw & Associates.

In the eleventh month of starting my business, I hit a financial low. I was unable to pay my personal bills and the bills for my business, and I was paying staff with bank overdraft. One day while driving to the office, I spoke out loud to God. I spoke the same thoughts I had had for weeks. On June 1, 2016, I told God exactly what I wanted to make that month. On June 11, I checked the bank account (just like I did every morning during the rough time), and I had not only made what I had claimed and more, but we weren't even halfway through the month. That scared me. Whoa! I had said out loud what I had been thinking for weeks, and within less than two weeks, I had manifested it. My heart wanted to keep the currency flowing (the manifestation flow), but my mind was afraid that maybe it wouldn't happen again. Have you ever been there? Can you recall when you wanted or needed something and within a short period of time, you were blessed to receive it? How did it make you feel? Isn't this exactly what He tells us to do in Matthew 7:7? "Ask and it will be given to you; seek and you will find; knock and the door will be opened to you."

Why then is it so difficult for us to simply follow what has been instructed? Often we are raised with blinders. We are taught to do the right thing according to societal standards. Think about it. How often are you told to tell the truth? Yet when you are having a bad day and someone asks how your day is, often your response is very polite—and a lie! Because you are doing the right thing. You are giving the one asking a pleasing response, but not the truth. Well I believe the same is true of our Bible teaching and upbringing. We know the scripture, ask, seek, and knock. Yet we do not feel deserving enough to go before God and ask for our needs.

Eventually, I realized the fear was a part of my limited belief system, and now I boldly go before the throne. Ouch! Even that sounds like I am doing something wrong, doesn't it? Refer to Hebrews 4:16 NIV: "Let us approach God's throne of grace with confidence, so that we may receive mercy and find grace to help us in our time of need." So what if you boldly go before the throne to ask (out loud) that God helps you to begin eliminating your limited beliefs and replacing them with courage to take every need and desire to Him?

It can be difficult to start a business, and you want your family and friends to support you. I did too and I felt really alone when I wasn't getting the support I needed, especially from close family members. Almost immediately, you want to play the role of the victim, thinking thoughts like, "This is why it is so hard to ______" (you can finish that line). The reality is, often, even your closest family will not support you in the way you expect, but I can tell you who will. When you are walking in your purpose, the resources, the people, the finances, the knowhow, and everything you need will *always arrive*. The resources you need will fall into your lap. Strength to endure sleepless nights will come effortlessly. Divine guidance will elevate you without the fear of falling or failing.

Six months after my financial low, I was able to move my business from a 300-square-foot office space, where we worked three to an office, into an office complex with three separate offices with room for growth. I allowed this to happen because I believed God for big things. I was not afraid to be bold in my asking.

It is also important to note that in your asking, remember to remain humble. When blessings come, you don't want to miss out on them because of pride. During the initial startup of the business, my personal finances were extremely limited and all of the income generated in the business stayed in the business. I was unable to buy new clothes, but God sent them anyway. When a friend came to me with a bag full of gently used business wear, I could have been too proud to accept them and could have missed out on the blessings, but I remained humble.

When I was exhausted from working eighty hours a week in the business, coming home late at night to finish homework with my eight-year-old, and trying to decide if I would have time to feed the kids before bedtime or if it would be another fast food night that I couldn't afford, I just wanted to quit. I wanted to give up and throw in the towel. I needed help, and help was not around.

One evening, I sent my adult daughter a message letting her know I couldn't do it anymore. Crying out to God, I just needed help. Less than two weeks later, help came knocking on my door. A friend of mine arranged a plan with her housekeepers to come to my house. One would clean while the other organized. Not only did I get the help I needed with my home, but I got so much more. I gained a friend and received the help I needed with my children: home-cooked meals twice a week and assistance with the day-to-day responsibilities of taking care of my home, from making a grocery list to paying bills. I received more than I could have ever imagined.

You don't know how your blessings will come or in what package they will arrive, so remain open to receive. Wouldn't it have been a shame if I had said to my friend, "Oh I don't need any help"? I would have missed out on all that I was asking God for at that time and a friendship that means so much to me. Do not be too proud and miss all the blessings God has in store for you. Be bold in your asking. Go big, ask for all that your mind can imagine, and always remain humble and open to receive the blessing.

In closing, I would like to prompt you to remember that the power of life and death lies in the power of your tongue. We are not merely to think our thoughts; we need to speak them aloud. Remember, He is waiting on you. He wants to answer your every prayer request. So as you are building your empire, don't be afraid to move beyond the comforts of what you have been taught and experience all the greatness of who God is and what He is ready to bless you with when you allow Him to work through you.

My Drive Is the Catalyst for My Success

Ranelli Williams

Being an entrepreneur is not an easy journey. It requires tenacity and dedication. It requires a desire, a determination, and a drive to win that everyone is not willing to push through. It requires faith to know that even when you do not see the full staircase, you still take the first step.

I started out in life with the odds against me. My mom was a twenty-one-year-old single mom who was just starting out in her career as a nurse. She still had much to learn as a nurse and had to prove herself in her profession while taking care of a little girl on her own. Thank God for her drive to succeed and to make a better life for me and my brother than she had growing up. My mom was and still is a very hard worker and was determined to win.

When you are willing to go to battle for what you want in accordance with God's will for your life, God will go to battle with you. And He did for my mom. He sent her my grandparents, my father's parents, who were always ready to babysit and kept me for months at a time when she worked the night shift. When I was a teenager, we moved to the United States from Montserrat, and my mother decided that she would pay my way through undergraduate school in cash so I would not have a student loan. Watching her sacrifice any form of social life and experience many sleepless nights as she worked two jobs, I could not help but be eternally grateful, and needless to say, I inherited some of that drive from her.

Although my dad was not in my household, he was always in my life. At the age of about ten, I watched him start his bakery from scratch and build it into a thriving business, which I worked in as a teenager. Today, more than thirty years later, it is still standing and is one of the premier bakeries on the island of Montserrat. My dad started as a parallelpreneur, working as the chief pharmacist at Glendon Hospital on Montserrat while building his business. A few years later, he was able to walk away from his job to work full-time in the business. That impressed me even as a young girl, and I decided I wanted to own my own business one day. I had no idea when, what that business would be, or how it would happen, but it was something I knew I would pursue one day.

I graduated from Borough of Manhattan Community College, City University of New York, with a degree in business management. However, as I went through my accounting classes, I realized my love for accounting, so I decided accounting would be my major when I transferred to a four-year college. Mirroring my mom's work ethic, I worked part-time for the next two years as I went to school full-time to complete my bachelor's.

After graduating with my BBA in accounting from Baruch College, City University of New York, I landed my first accounting job as a junior accountant with payroll and accounts payable duties. The company I worked for had a tuition reimbursement program and, learning early never to waste an opportunity, I immediately registered for the MBA program at Baruch College. I worked full-time while attending school part-time. Four years later, I had my MBA under my belt. Most people would think it was a great accomplishment and be satisfied to live the status quo, but remember the drive I got from my parents? I wanted more. I was ready to advance in my career and it was not happening fast enough in my job at the time. I started looking for new job opportunities and quickly realized that my undergraduate in accounting coupled with my MBA were great for certain positions, but the jobs I really wanted required a certified public accounting (CPA) license.

Yep, you guessed correctly. I immediately enrolled in a CPA review course and spent the next year and a half studying and taking the CPA exam. Once I passed the exam, the license was not immediate. I did not have the auditing experience necessary to gain my license, so I applied to many public accounting companies where I could get the auditing experience I needed. It was a very competitive market, so getting in the door was not easy, but what I had going for me was my drive to make it happen and God on my side.

One day, it dawned on me that I had a contact in one of the Big Four accounting firms. Gaining Big Four accounting experience would be a big boost for my accounting career. This experience was every accountant's dream and what the major companies were looking for and would pay premium dollars for in a candidate. I had to make it happen. I made a few phone calls, got my resume in the right hands, and got the interview that I was fighting to get for months. I knew that once I had that open-ing, I could not mess it up. I reached out to a few contacts for tips on interviewing with that type of firm. I prepared and practiced, practiced and prepared.

The day of the interview, I was ready and knocked it out of the ballpark. I was offered the job the same day and although I did not have audit experience, because I had accounting experi-ence, I was brought in as a second year with supervisory respon-sibilities over the first years.

Life was great. I worked hard, gained great experience, and fostered some relationships that I still have today. I worked in public accounting for three years, learned a whole lot about ac-counting and auditing, became a CPA in the process, and then moved on to an internal audit role in a large private company. I really enjoyed the role, I was well paid, and I learned much of what I know today about business processes. Walking into a department in a short space of time, learning what they do, developing audit procedures to determine if they had the right policies and procedures in place to mitigate possible risks, de-termining whether they were adhering to these policies and procedures, and offering recommendations for any issues iden-tified, prepared me for business ownership.

Once my husband lost his job in 2010 and was home for more than a year, we decided to turn the little side hustle we did preparing taxes for family and friends into a legitimate busi-ness. When life throws you lemons, you make lemonade. So in 2012, we registered and started ERJ Services, LLC. With my great income and my husband building the business, we were okay. I knew that one day I would join him in the business.

At that time, I was in a position that I was not quite happy with. My internal audit position was eliminated and while I found a position within the same company that was great pay and the managerial position I was seeking, I soon realized it was not the place for me. I was making good money and working from home most of the time, but miserable in the position. My prayer was that God would show us a way to grow our business to the point where I could replace the income I made on my job and be able to walk away. However, I was not aggressive enough in my actions. We have to remember that the Bible says, "Faith by itself, if it is not accompanied by action, is dead" (James 2:17 NIV). My actions were not backing up my prayers. Remember, I said the money was good, so although I was miserable, I was comfortable. But we have to step out of our comfort zones if we are going to make our goals happen.

In November 2014, I received a call from my employer and was informed that my services were no longer needed. My severance package along with the unemployment I received gave us about eight months to get things in place financially. We moved from being just a tax practice to providing bookkeeping and accounting services as well. Now, we were both full-time in the business—a huge step of faith. But every step of the way, God was with us. Within three months of going full-time in the business, we were recommended as accountants to a company who is now our largest accounting client. However, even with that client, we faced great financial hardship. We went from a six-figure income that I was making to about a quarter of that income in a year. How were we to pay our bills? Only by the grace of God are we still standing, and nothing has been repossessed.

I want to digress a bit to talk about relationships. Relationships are so vital to our growth in business and life in general. While at my last job, I connected with various mentors, but one in particular always shared books with me to read. One of the books she shared with me was *Monday Morning Motivation.* In that book, I learned so much about the importance of having mentors and coaches who have traveled the path you are on to guide you along the way. And not only connecting with them but fostering those relationships and bringing value to them as well. I started connecting with mentors and coaches, all of whom I learned something from. One encouraged me to overcome my fears, which led me to writing my book. Another led me to the connections that made writing and publishing the book possible. Another introduced me to Dave Ramsey's Financial Peace University, which my husband and I went through and then became facilitators for.

In 2015, I met Aprille Franks-Hunt, and she became my business coach. That was a huge leap of faith financially, but it significantly changed the game for me and our business. I know it was a God connection because God sure knows how to place the right people in our paths at the opportune time. I learned so many valuable lessons, connected with numerous individuals in ministry and business who have since become strategic partners, and just began to take bold steps in things that I never thought I would. We implemented a plan we developed to double our tax practice. We gained new bookkeeping clients. I connected with someone who is now my cohost of an annual conference we hold in the Poconos for faith-based women in business. I rereleased my book and included the testimonies of some amazing women of God, some of whom I developed relationships with and am collaborating with on other things. I learned how to pitch myself to be featured in the media and have been featured on Forbes. com, Madam Noire, and CocoaFab. This all happened because I had enough faith to make an uncomfortable move, and as a result, God opened the doors that were waiting for me all along. And I know there's more where that came from.

This gave me great confidence to step out and lead this book collaboration effort. I have truly learned the meaning of community, relationship building, and collaborations, which in turn lead to opportunities for business growth. The journey has just begun. I am nowhere near what I know is possible through my heavenly Father, but what I do know is that one leap of faith will lead to a lifetime of learning and exponential growth in your life and business. That is what has happened and is continuing to happen for me. And that is what can happen for you too. Bold moves provide big blessings.

Be bold!

DOCTORAL FEAT

*Six Faith Walkers Share Their Commitment
to Completing Their Terminal Degrees*

Stuck in the Middle

Dr. William Irish-O'Brien

I am a registered nurse currently employed as director of nursing in a facility in the Bronx, New York. I started nursing over thirty years ago, so I am well into the latter end of my time in this profession. I migrated to the United States almost twenty-eight years ago, seeking a life that was different from what I had previously known.

Over the years and after much hard work, I achieved many successes. These areas of success have been stepping stones in my spiritual walk. With each success, I have learned to trust in the great "I AM." This was not always easy. Life has a way of throwing you curve balls, and in these situations, your faith is tested beyond belief, but we will talk about the testing times later.

Easy times are not guaranteed to any specific person. Every human goes through difficult times, and during those times, the absence of faith increases the intensity of the adverse experience. I was not content to just be. I was always driven. I wanted more, to be more, for deep inside, I felt there was something great just waiting for the right moment to break through. I could feel it day after day, and I knew that some day in the future my true purpose would be manifested.

My life's journey took me through several wonderful places that I may not have experienced if I had not learned to trust God. Trusting was not always an easy thing for me to do. My self-reliance sometimes got in the way, and periodically I have had to hit my reset button to realign my footsteps according to His purpose and His will. Over time, I have learned that trust is not just a word but a mindset that requires intentional action and humbly seeking the direction of the heavenly father.

I continued along my path, seeking new experiences, meeting new people, and appreciating the changing landscape of my journey. Life is by no means perfect, but you learn to live with what you have. Sometimes all you can do is just be right where you are.

My journey took me though the process of studying and eventually succeeding in achieving my MBA. Then I had the idea that I wanted to fulfill a lifelong dream of achieving a doctoral degree. There was no way I would have known that this journey would test me to my limit. I had no idea that I would be stuck in the middle of completing this doctoral journey. Everything was going well, moving according to my plan. Suddenly I was stuck, stomped, completely frozen.

I started my doctoral journey with excitement. I was totally pumped and ready to go. I sailed through the initial stages of the program with a smile on my face. This was easy, I thought. I took my courses, completed my assignments, and took part in the discussions. I was not stressed, but then I started to observe that the work was becoming more intense and the requirements were increasingly complex, involving greater research and intricate analysis.

The routine requirements of the doctoral journey fell into place, and I did what was required with outstanding results. I started working on my manuscript, and I completed the required chapters, learning as I went how to improve my research abilities and how to format the document. The information I gathered during the time I spent conducting the study offered me insight into the perspectives of the nurses who participated. I was simply amazed at the commonality of the similar thread running through the dialogue. The need for changes in nursing education and the need to ensure nurse executives in long-term care facilities acquire training in business education were evident as I spoke with the participants. Even more amazing was that those who participated in the study did not know each other and were interviewed at varied times. Yet the sentiment was the same. I completed the research and did the required analysis. The dissertation was finally complete and the time came to submit it to the Quality Review Board. I just knew for certain that I submitted great work and my dissertation was going to sail through with flying colors and horns blaring.

The results came back with multiple edits that needed to be done. My heart fell to my feet. I became angry, but I did not know with whom I was supposed to be angry. I internalized the rejection of my work and became stuck. I could not move forward. I lost the zeal. I had poured by blood and sweat into this doctoral journey and now I was stuck. I had set my deadline when I wanted to complete this doctoral journey and any interruption to that schedule would throw my plan off schedule.

Time went by and I did not address the required edits. I could not focus on the work. I could not summon the energy to move forward. I became angry with myself. I was smart, and I knew what to do, so why was I not moving forward? I questioned God's oversight. He knew I needed this. How could He let me down so badly? This was a doctoral journey for crying out loud! I was doing great in all other areas, but in this one area, I was stumped.

The questioning of myself further plunged me into that abyss of self-doubt. The more I tried to find the answers within myself, the more I felt stuck, like a car stuck in the mud on a rainy day. My wheels were spinning, but I was not going anywhere. Where I was in my particular journey did not make sense.

But I still went to work and functioned effectively. Like a good father, I took care of my son. All was going well except this particular area of my life. This feeling of defeat persisted for a long while. There were those who supported me and would ask how the program was progressing. I would just say I was "hanging in there." It was difficult to articulate the bump in my journey. I did not know how to explain to those who were familiar with my program that I was in the middle of a desert experience; that the land of my personal experience was dry and parched.

Not being able to identify the root cause of my problem caused me further angst. The inability to move resulted in me withdrawing inside myself. I would go to church and pray to God to do for me what I could not do for myself, to make the crooked path straight, to help me get beyond this drought. Indeed, I felt that my experience was akin to wandering in a barren land.

The inability to move forward can be a concerning experience. I did not like how I was feeling. I questioned my abilities, specifically my intellectual abilities. I knew where I needed to go. I was very much aware of what the outcome of my journey would be. I just needed to figure out how to get there. I needed to understand what had happened and how to move beyond this desert experience.

I slowly began to refocus, and I heard the voice of one of my professors reiterating that a student must finish the program. Not to finish would foster a constant shadow of incompletion. That made me uncomfortable. I was not a quitter. I was from a strong family who worked hard. I knew nothing else. My great-grandmother, who raised me, was the epitome of strength and stick-to-it-iveness. My great-grandmother was a fearless woman of faith. She could face giants and trample them, and I needed a dose of what she had. I knew I was strong because I had to be during my early years, and I knew that, deep within, I had an untapped reservoir of energy, hope, and faith. I needed to tap into this reservoir.

Slowly, my mind wandered to a text in the Bible that offered, if I put my hand to the plow and take it back, I am not worthy (Luke 9:62). I knew I would never be satisfied with not completing this doctoral journey. One day, I woke up and I knew without a doubt I had to go back to the drawing board and finish what I started. This awareness was not dramatic. It just started as a nagging irritation that would not leave me alone. Looking back, I now realized that God was gently pushing me back on track.

With renewed energy, I started back on my journey. I worked diligently on the edits. I did everything I was supposed to do. I still was not where I wanted to be, but I was chipping away at the obstacles in my path. The constant question in my head was,

"How can I eat this elephant?" and the answer came back loud and clear in my head: "one bite at a time."

Obstacles provide new pathways for growth and development. I learned that the faith walker must be bold and fearless, but boldness does not always come in a dramatic fashion with loud noises for effect as in Hollywood blockbuster movies. Boldness does not always take center stage. Boldness can come through the quietness of renewed strength. The intentional act of relying completely on the promises of God reinforces the faith walker with bonds of spiritual steel.

Being bold requires keen perception. The ability to recognize opportunities are essential. One cannot be bold without taking action and a leap of faith. Being bold is not a stand-alone concept, and it is the intentional action of boldness that results in success.

I knew I was on the right path when I saw that the more I relied on the promises of God, the more I accomplished. The ever-constant reminder that God will be with me always, even unto the end of the world (Matthew 28:20), charged my batteries. The amazing thing was, when I started to work on my edits, I realized they were not that bad! But even as I gained this new perspective, I learned all over again that my timeline was not God's timeline. So many times we unconsciously demand that God comes through on our schedule. God comes at the moment that he needs to come, not before, not after! The quiet awareness of my reawakening was contingent on my relationship with God and my willingness to boldly trust Him even when I could not understand how He was working things out. I realized that

I will never figure out the complexities of my God. I just have to be a faith walker.

After a year, I completed my edits and resubmitted my dissertation, and won't you know—it was again returned for more edits. This time, my response was so different. I actually laughed to myself. My journey was akin to every other doctoral journey. There are multiple rewrites and reviews. There are critiques and quality reviews to ensure the best work is produced, but here I am today, Dr. William Irish-O'Brien. When we boldly step out on the wings of faith, we need no exit strategy.

The journey was not the issue. The issue was my perspective and my level of faith in myself, in the doctoral journey, and in God. With each review, I noticed my dissertation was being transformed into a respectable document worthy to be authored by a doctoral candidate who walks with the heavenly father. The object lesson for me was that as we are tested and tried, we go through a period of refinement and ultimately come through so much better than before.

I walk not by my physical sight but by the faith in the great "I AM." Sometimes the lessons to be learned are not in the actual problem but in the path leading to the problem. If we pay attention to the potholes in the road, the journey will be smoother. As I continued to work on my dissertation, I saw a parallel to my walk with God. As each review of the document yielded a higher quality product, each obstacle in my path improved my relationship with God and made me a better man. This is the result of the refiner's fire.

Looking back on my doctoral journey, I can clearly see the hand of God working for my good. I stand on the promises that

God's faithfulness is concrete. It is immovable, unshakable, and everlasting. At times it can be very hard to see the hand of God when one is going through the desert experience. Do not despair; it does not matter how dark your individual desert experience is—the morning will come. Problems look so much worse during the night, but the morning brings new light and new awareness as you face the obstacles. My prayer for you is that you will persevere no matter what obstacles are in your way. The extent of your visual field is minor compared to God's view of the universe.

There Is Always Hope

Dr. Bernice A. Bramble

I was born on the island of Montserrat, a British colony in the Eastern Caribbean. My father was a farmer and died suddenly in my early teens. My mother had a difficult task of being the sole provider for eleven children.

One day, my mother said, "Your father isn't feeling well and I am taking him to see a doctor." As the days of his hospitalization went by, I could see the increasing distress in my mother. "According to the doctor," she said, "he is not getting any better."

What exactly that meant was unclear to me because children were taught to listen and not to question adults. Then, one week after he was hospitalized, before the break of dawn, a knock on the bedroom window aroused us from our sleep. When I heard the sound, my heart skipped a beat. My sixth sense alerted me of the ominous sign. It was our neighbor, who came to convey the sad news that our beloved father had died. The news was both mind blowing and earth shattering. My life was transformed that day.

My father had planted many positive seeds in my life. I can still recall when he told me I would go to college and get a bachelor's degree. I never understood the implications of this declaration, but the memory was etched in my mind. The entire family was shocked by the tragic news. It was surreal and I felt a deep sense of sorrow. Many questions occupied my thoughts. The challenges ahead were real.

Throughout my life, thoughts of my father were continuously present. The expectations he had for me engrossed my every waking second and provided the stimulus that motivated me to follow my divine destiny.

My mother grew up in a Methodist family. She was raised in an environment wrapped within the culture of the "Protestant work ethic," and spent her entire life following the lessons and aphorisms of her belief. My mother believed that good character, hard work, strength of mind, and unbridled faith were the fundamentals that would reap great rewards.

She was a "jack of all trades" but worked mainly as a peddler. Her working days were long and tiresome while she strived to do what was necessary to put food on the table. She followed this process six days a week. On Sundays, we went to church. Her code for living in every situation of her life, hardship, and harvest, was personified in her favorite scripture, "I will bless the Lord at all times: His praise shall continually be in my mouth" (Psalm 34:1 KJV). She felt that God should always be praised in every circumstance. Like Joshua (24:15), she dutifully established, "As for me and my house we will serve the Lord."

My mother gave me the gifts of fortitude, faith, philosophy, and unconditional love. "God is in the midst," she would say. I would leave for school without lunch money, and she would pat me on the head and say, "God does not make mistakes; He sends mouth and He also sends bread." When it really seemed as if she would never be able to make ends meet, she would say, "He will make a way even where there is no way." I felt encouraged by my mother's affirmations.

Growing up in abject poverty shaped me as a person. Psalms 46:1, "I will lift up mine eyes unto the hills from whence cometh my help," provided the encouragement I needed. However, my self-assurance was grounded in Mark 11:23 ESV: "Truly, I say to you, whoever says to this mountain, 'Be taken up and thrown into the sea,' and does not doubt in his heart, but believes that what he says will come to pass, it will be done for him." I felt confident that God created me and wanted me to live in the bold delight of knowing that exercising faith could literally move mountains. This unwavering trust undergirded and fortified me for the journey that I followed from poverty to the pinnacle of success. Along the way, I succeeded in the proficiencies and requirements to reach the acme of education and obtain a PhD.

The Early Years

In my youthful days, my favorite activity was climbing trees. Reaching the top of a tree gave me a sense of accomplishment, and sitting in the hollow where the limbs met the trunk felt like heaven. The encounter not only gave me a sense of authority; it also offered me an opportunity for seclusion and silence, a chance to think, and to get away from the chaos and disorder that was the distinct character of a crowded household. The presence of God in my life was revealed to me while sitting in my favorite spot, a rainfall tree that shaded our house. I was memorizing a Bible verse for Sunday school. The passage was taken from Jeremiah 29:11 NIV, "'For I know the plans I have for you,' declares the Lord, 'plans to prosper you and not to harm you, plans to give you hope and a future.'"

I had a sudden realization that God knew me personally, had a design for my life, and was willing to allow me to find hope in Him. Moreover, this epiphany made me appreciate I was an individual with personal attitudes, hopes, and desires. I understood that I could rely on the promises of God and I knew that He would order my development and control the course of my life. At that moment, I placed my childlike faith in Jesus Christ and began to embrace my divine providence. Subsequently, I was able to acknowledge the connection and complete the deduction. If God is all-powerful, since He made me in His own image, I am also powerful.

PREPARATION FOR LIFE

In primary school, the daily gathering of our class was under a shady tree at the entrance of the school. The teacher stood at the front: "Students, form rows." The tallest students stood in the back row; the smallest stood in the front. The teacher continued her instructions: "All stand straight; feet together, elbows bent, and forearms bent at the level of the waist, palms facing up." The teacher walked across the front row, then to the back row, examining each student as she strolled along, inspecting our hair, garb, hands, nails, and feet. "Cleanliness is next to Godliness," she said with each step.

I thought to myself, "This teacher is powerful. When I grow up I want to be just like her."

The daily declarations followed: "Students, one at a time, come to the front of the class and tell your classmates what you want to be when you grow up."

As each pupil stood in the front of the class, there were echoes of, "I want to be a nurse," "I want to be a policeman," "I want to be a butcher," "I want to be a farmer." Then it was my turn.

"I want to be a teacher," I said meekly.

The student standing directly in front of me sighed and said, "Yeah right, you can't be no teacher."

"Yes I can!" I shouted.

The monitor observed the discourse and informed the teacher. When we got back to the classroom, both of us were asked to stand in the corner on one leg for ten minutes. It was my first encounter with injustice. I didn't understand the reason for punishment. After all, I was only stating my aspiration. Then and there, I decided I would never lose sight of my aspiration of becoming a teacher.

SPEAK THE DREAM INTO BEING

Teaching was in my spirit, and I sincerely believed that I could make the leap of faith with God's grace. He had given me the talent of believing that I could design the life I wanted, and I knew that it was His will that I succeed. This awareness quickly became a passion, which captured my every waking moment. I steadfastly visualized the dream in my heart and in my mind. I knew I could change the course of my life if I learned the principles that governed success.

I was convinced that academic success could make a difference in the course of my life. I saw the benefits of a good education all around me. It seemed like a natural progression. Educated people went to high school, they obtained degrees of higher learning, and they had "good" jobs, and were privileged.

They were pillars of the community. Those positive foundations provided proof and motivation for me, so I became an eager learner. The groundwork was set; seeds of encouragement were planted and watered.

What the Mind Visualizes, It Can also Realize

Attending high school was the hallmark of a far-reaching education. For me, there were many hurdles to overcome. I could get into high school by obtaining either a scholarship or by paying school fees. I thought to myself, I have already passed the scholarship age because I was never given the opportunity to write the entrance exam at the approved age.

The principal's response to my request to take the entrance examination was, "Your mother cannot afford to pay." That was the truth. That kind of education was beyond my family's meager financial resources. However, the principal's veracity did not hinder my tenacity. The situation was illogical. But I chose to believe God.

Scriptures validate the supremacy of our thoughts, the influence of the mind, and the authority we have over our own lives. With the power of the spoken word, we can accurately speak into existence the life we desire. I understood that my dream was peculiar and would require extraordinary assistance. My prayers were answered and I was granted "unmerited favor." God blessed me with an amazing teacher who gave me free lessons so that I could successfully pass the entrance examination. I graduated high school with distinction six years later, and the day after I graduated from high school, I was chosen to teach at an elementary school.

MOVING MOUNTAINS, FULFILLING DREAMS

Teaching was a stepping stone on the journey to my actual vocation, so after teaching for two years, I decided that becoming a nurse was the road I ought to travel. My older sister persuaded me to follow this path.

"You could be a nurse," she told me. "As a nurse, you could make a significant difference in people's lives." She added, "You could go to the United Kingdom for training, and then you would be just as qualified as the matron at the hospital."

I believed her. Our mother's best friend was a nurse and she helped us out in many ways. But the idea was unimaginable. A gnawing voice in my head kept repeating, how will you get to the United Kingdom? In the stillness of my thoughts, a gentle quiet voice reminded me, "I will lift up mine eyes unto the hills from whence cometh my help" (Psalms 121:1). The gnawing voice was subdued. The mountains in the background that adorned the island stood covered in mist. Then suddenly the mist lifted and the rain started to fall. It was both poetic and prophetic.

Three years later, I was accepted into nursing school and journeyed to the metropolis of London. Four and a half years later, I graduated with certifications in nursing and midwifery. I received a very comprehensive preparation during my training, which fully equipped me to follow the path that God had crafted for me.

A LIFE OF SERVICE

Galatians 6:9 ISV declares, "Let's not get tired of doing what is good, for at the right time we will reap a harvest—if we do not give up." This scripture cautions us to carry out our duties meticulously and to the best of our ability. The concept supports my goal for living, which is to make a meaningful difference in the lives of all the individuals I have had the opportunity to serve. I have been a nurse for over forty-five years and have a passion for bedside nursing. I earnestly believe that in that setting, I can make a definite distinction in the lives of patients, their families, and the community at large.

THE SKY IS THE LIMIT

The forty-plus years that I have spent carrying out bedside nursing exposed me to the plight of senior nurses and made me realize it was time to move on to the next chapter of my life. I always sought counsel from the word of God when looking for direction. While examining, I found out there was no theological standard in reference to retirement. But rather, as an individual reaches a certain milestone, the focus may change, but the individual's life work of service never changes. With this endorsement, I decided to go back to school to obtain a PhD in human services.

I made the decision to continue my education based on Philippians 1:6 WBT: "Being confident of this very thing, that he who hath begun a good work in you, will perform it until the day of Jesus Christ." I wanted to make a professional transition. Specifically, I wanted to bring attention to the plight of senior nurses who have spent a lifetime at the bedside. I had been out of school for over fifteen years and I was faced with a vertical learning curve. There were many setbacks, but I stayed steadfast, submissive, and systematic. Most importantly, I stayed the course and won the race. Six years later, I graduated Magna Cum Laude with a PhD in human services, majoring in healthcare administration.

KEEP ON BELIEVING

I was born with special talents, given to me by my Heavenly Father to equip me to accomplish His purpose in my life. As I lived from day to day, I was presented with many confronts. I kept reminding myself that all things were possible if I trusted God.

In spite of the hurdles in life, there is always hope, and the choice to believe that the best things can and will happen. The understanding that our dreams can become authentic can truly usher us through the storms of life to our God-given purpose.

I acknowledge God's presence in my life and have aligned myself with His power and His will. I believe that His promises are real and that He will never fail me. I was able to overcome the obstacles that were obstructing my path by recognizing that challenges bring forth opportunities. Taking these opportunities led me to my God-given determination. I have continuously experienced the blessings of God throughout my life. And I am a true living testimony of His amazing grace and mercy. Because of my experiences, I truly believe that we can all be victorious in becoming the person God wants us to be. How about you? If you believe that God does extraordinary things with ordinary people, then you are on the right track.

Speaking Victory over My Qualms

Dr. Garrett Ingram

On October 6, 2016, I received a phone call from Mrs. Ranelli Williams, and she expressed her interest in me writing a chapter in her next book collaboration. We discussed the foundation of this collective project, which involved individuals sharing their unique story of stepping out in faith, overcoming adversity, and maintaining momentum, all while achieving desired goals. This is my story of how my relationship with Jesus guided my determination and drive with achieving a PhD. My hope is that this chapter will provide graduate students with holistic empowerment (e.g., positive reinforcement, positive psychology, mindfulness) to purposely guide you with successfully overcoming obstacles and completing your doctoral journeys. So remember to be positive, for someone is always praying you up.

In March 2016, I graduated from Capella University with a PhD. My field of study is advanced studies of human behavior. I am also an Elder at Mount Pocono Temple of Seventh-Day Adventists, meaning I have taken an active role in teaching my congregation about the life of Jesus Christ and how to apply biblical principles in their Christian walk. My goal is to help church members gain prosperity while reaching their highest of heights in all aspects of their lives.

My spiritual journey has allowed me to gain insight with the understanding that various setbacks were strategically placed along my path to purposely push me to critically analyze my position. These challenging tasks (e.g., completing assignments due the same day, completing multiple reading assignments) helped me see the bigger picture of perceiving all forms of setbacks as object lessons for overcoming adversity, gaining resiliency, and obtaining the drive to successfully complete this journey. Overall, my doctoral journey has been a wonderful experience of growth and expansion as well as a stimulating adventure during which I had to challenge my own beliefs, think outside of my mind box, and learn to respond favorably to constructive criticism.

The Foundation of My Doctoral Journey

During July of 2011, I had a telephone conversation with a friend, whom I had located through social media. During 1988, we were study partners during our graduate years at John Jay College, where we received our master's degrees in forensic psychology. I had not spoken to my friend in twenty-three years so we had a lot of catching up to do. During our conversation, my friend informed me she was pursuing an online PhD in psychology from Capella University. I was very intrigued as I also had an interest in pursuing a PhD, so I explored the PhD programs at Capella University to see if there was a program that captivated my interest.

I was specifically looking for a program that combined psychology, spirituality, behavior, eating disorders, holistic growth and development, resiliency, child abuse, and maltreatment. I found an online PhD program in advanced studies of human behavior, which captured the above mentioned topics. Subsequently, I enrolled in the PhD program and registered for my first class to begin September 2011.

During orientation, the instructor said that less than 2 percent of students were able to successfully complete their doctoral journeys. The instructor revealed writing skills, creative thinking, family conflict, relationship issues, family commitment, and job responsibilities were some of the reasons students weren't able to complete their doctorate. The instructor further specified that students must maintain momentum, be proactive, successfully manage their responsibilities, and use their time wisely in order to complete their reading assignments, classwork responsibilities, and the many papers assigned throughout each semester.

After orientation, I meditated on the daunting tasks needed to complete this program and had reservations on whether I could successfully complete this journey while also spending quality time with my family, maintaining my job responsibilities, and attending to my church duties. I further thought about the amount of time I would have to spend doing research, completing assignments, and conducting reading tasks. My anxiety levels greatly increased and I considered withdrawing from the program. However, I considered one of my favorite Bible quotes, spoken by the Apostle Paul: "I can do all things through Christ which strengtheneth me" (Philippians 4:13 KJV). Immediately,

I considered this doctoral journey to be a challenge I could conquer. I felt optimistic, and the prayers from my family and church family gave me endurance, perseverance, and strength to successfully complete this monumental journey.

Object Lessons

I further considered my doctoral journey to be a rewarding adventure, with many wonderful object lessons of trials and tribulations that some may perceive as dross infused on a diamond. But I believed the successes received with overcoming adversity would transform me into a beacon of light designed to inspire others to succeed in their studies too. Malachi said Jesus is "a refiner and purifier of silver: and he shall purify the sons of Levi, and purge them as gold and silver, that they may offer unto the Lord an offering in righteousness" (Malachi 3:3 KJV). Before I started this doctoral journey, I had decided to have an optimistic demeanor and to use trying circumstances as opportunities to strengthen my resiliency, which would allow me to share my experiences with fellow doctoral students with the goal of helping them persevere in their academic studies.

Jesus says "Let your light so shine before men, that they may see your good works, and glorify your Father which is in heaven." (Matthew 5:16 KJV). So no matter what your circumstances are, your trials and tribulations are opportunities for growth and development, not only for you but for all others who have the opportunity of hearing your testimony of succeeding in the midst of adversity.

Additionally, my doctoral journey was parallel to my marital journey. Having overcome many storms during my sixteen years of marriage, I learned that a successful marriage is based on steadfast commitment, open communication, admission of faults, and the willingness to perceive circumstances from my spouse's lenses. This all provided a blueprint for my successful navigation through my doctoral journey.

Similarly, my doctoral journey can also be parallel to my spiritual journey, for there have been intervals of excitement and joy, as well as intervals of despair and gloom. Many times during my spiritual journey, I felt the weight of a piano on my shoulders due to the many pressing issues that taxed my strength and endurance. However, I kept pressing on, prayed, fasted, and received strength and support from my family and friends. Solomon concluded, "to everything *there is* a season, and a time to every purpose under the heaven," (Ecclesiastes 3:1 KJV). This text, along with many other texts located in this chapter that discuss various emotions a person can expect to experience along one's spiritual journey, provided me with encouragement and strengthened my resiliency with completing my doctoral journey, as I was able to reflect on my periods of stagnation as opportunities to channel constructive criticism into positive thoughts and behaviors.

One of the major obstacles I faced during the program was developing a heading for my dissertation. During this time of contemplating the title of my study, I experienced one of the many object lessons that gave me momentum to rise above the adversity. I had developed a title of my research, even before I had enrolled in doctoral studies, which was pleasing to my heart. However, my mentor recommended that I alter the title to ensure it aligned with my research methodology because it was not capturing the qualitative study I had planned to use in my dissertation. I agonized about this issue for two weeks before I was fully committed to changing my title, but once I changed the title, I was able to fully see its suitability.

Another object lesson that provided inspiration and fortitude was the two eastern hemlock evergreen trees standing majestically in the back of my house. Unlike the other trees, which lose their leaves during the fall and winter months, these two evergreen trees retain their leaves throughout the year. By watching these two trees stand boldly in the midst of the scorching sun, surviving many heavy winter storms, I learned to overcome life's storms and to maintain a proactive stance and positive demeanor while completing my coursework, completing the comprehensive examination, and finishing my dissertation.

During my journey, I learned to be joyful when I was experiencing highs and to critically examine my thoughts and behaviors when circumstances were not going as planned. Furthermore, during times when I had difficulty completing my classwork assignments, I remembered that the coursework was designed to test my faith, check my endurance, and challenge my ability to rise above adversity. So for all graduate students facing adversity in their studies, remember to be proactive and retain momentum, for there will be potholes specifically placed along your journey to help you master the competencies of your educational program.

Peter tells us in 1 Peter 4:12-13, "Beloved, think it not strange concerning the fiery trial which is to try you, as though some strange thing happened unto you: but rejoice, inasmuch as ye are partakers of Christ's sufferings; that, when his glory shall be revealed, ye may be glad also with exceeding joy." For graduate students who are facing similar circumstances in their academic adventures and who have considered discontinuing their studies, meditate on the notion of Jesus showering you with blessings by using your situation to help you see the bigger picture, by testing your faith to purposely heighten your thoughts, and by empowering you to complete your studies and share your experiences with others with the goal of inspiring others to complete their studies too.

CONCLUSION

For those students pursuing doctoral studies, remember that everyone's journey is different—some will have fewer obstacles while others may have to overcome a tremendous amount. Do not get discouraged if another student is able to finish before you. Furthermore, encourage yourself and speak victory over your situation, for greater is He that is in you, than He who is in the world. So have a wonderful day, keep pressing on, and remember to always demonstrate positive psychology.

Faith and Academics

Dr. Sylvia Ephraim

I believe that my story about my doctoral journey can motivate and encourage you (the readers) to go the extra mile to achieve your dream. My story is one of faith, and how my human side tried to interfere every step of the way, but my strong faith kept me moving. I can truly testify that with Christ in my vessel, I can smile at any storm. This is my reality, and it is true for anyone who believes.

My journey started after I decided to go back to school in January 2011 to pursue a doctoral degree at Capella University. Being the workaholic that I am, I decided also to pursue a post-master's certificate in college teaching. This was my first time taking all my courses online, and it took a lot of independent study. I completed this certificate in summer 2011 with all As, and started my doctoral journey at the same time. I had no issues as I completed the post-master's certification and the coursework for my PhD, but then problems arose during the dissertation phase, or the research process, of the program. I can testify that that was when my faith was tested and the hard work began.

Time management is a skill I learned a long time ago. I created my schedule each week and all that I planned to accomplish.

This schedule included not only my courses, but the things I had to do in my personal life. Everything had to be included on that schedule, such as my personal work at home, my schoolwork, and even the time allotted for my spiritual life. This included designating time for each chore, study, and preparation for youth biblical programs at my church. I encourage anyone who is planning to complete a graduate degree of any kind to create or develop a weekly schedule to manage his or her time. I can testify that it has helped me, and I believe it will help others as well.

While going through this process, I was the Adventist youth leader at my church, and was still very active on a daily prayer line at 5:30 a.m. I had all my sisters praying for me, and I worshipped and gave God the praises and honor He deserved. It is very important to put God first and to put everything in His hands. It took a lot of prayer on my part to complete this journey, and this is possible for anyone who truly trusts God. At times, you will be tested, and there are things that you will have to sacrifice. I had to miss family outings: some things I only attended for a few hours because I could not stay the allotted time. The key was following my schedule diligently, and it worked for completing my coursework. The next step in my journey was to complete a comprehensive exam of which I was only allowed two attempts.

The comprehensive exam is prepared by the school, and all I knew was that two of the questions would be from my area of interest where I would be conducting research. The third question would be a research question. These questions are essay type questions and must be completed in fourteen days. Two professors read your paper and both of them must give you a satisfactory grade or it will be given to a third reader, who is the deciding factor. I was very ecstatic but had some apprehension, especially when I heard so many had failed the exam. I started praying even more because I believe that nothing is impossible with the God I serve. I prayed and I asked God to take control, and to help me fulfill the dream my father and others had for me. I continued to ask my prayer line sisters to pray for me because much prayer, much power. I knew that I could not do this alone. It is so important to seek prayer from our friends and loved ones. I know that prayer gave me the sense of peace that I needed to take the exam.

I took the exam in February 2013 and both professors gave me outstanding reviews. I knew it was not me, but all God. I claimed God's promises that if I seek Him first, all other things will be added. This is my reality, and it can be true of anyone who seeks Him. Again, I gave God the praise, the honor, and the glory and kept on seeking Him for continued peace and success.

During the two-week break after completing the comprehensive exam, I completed the first section of my research plan; then I took the collaborative institutional training initiative (CITI). This is a coursework requirement that is needed if one's research includes human participants, and it has a pass mark of 85 percent. I took eleven modules and passed all with a grade of 100 percent. I did this to keep ahead of the game, so to speak. In addition, I took a bold step and wrote to a professor, asking her to be my mentor. I did this because I heard a friend say that the professor was a Christian (a child of God). Now, the school selects your mentor, but when I asked the professor and she agreed, I wrote the school (again, doing this with faith and prayer), and I was allowed to have her as my mentor. This was truly all God, and I learned that anything is possible if we have faith and trust in Him. Again, I gave God the glory.

When school reopened, I sought approval for the section that I had completed for my research plan. My mentor had a conference in Pennsylvania and wanted me to meet with her there to discuss what I had submitted to her. During our meeting, she explained how the research plan should be completed. Everything was going well until she received an email message with an issue of plagiarism by another student. My mentor started speaking to me in a very unpleasant manner. I sat there quietly, my eyes filling with tears because I was shocked by her behavior. Then she composed herself and apologized.

I knew my mentor overacted because of one student's mistake, and because I was the one present, I was given the negative behavior. Yet at the same, this was our first meeting, and I felt that the reaction toward me was unpleasant. I felt hurt, but it motivated me to work as hard as possible to prove to my mentor that not all students are the same. I left there shaken and in fear of the negative behavior I had experienced. I wondered if I would have to deal with the negative behavior as we continued working together.

I told my husband that I didn't know what I had gotten myself into, and I didn't think I wanted to continue. My husband is always very soothing with his speeches, and he told me that I could not let one mishap deter me; God had been working thus far, and He would continue to work on my behalf. Those words echoed in my mind and brought back my peace. Sometimes in life, we all need reassurance or words of hope from someone.

I continued my journey and made the necessary changes from the feedback I had received. I submitted it to my mentor and got her approval. My plan then went to the chair of the business department for her approval. Once it was approved I submitted it to the CITI program and got approval for my second milestone. I proceeded to complete the following six sections of the research plan and sent it for approval. I got approval from my mentor and one of my committee members, but the other committee member never responded. Each person has fourteen days to return a response, and that time had passed. My faith started to waiver a little because the quarter was going to finish, and I did not have the third approval. I started emailing him, and then eventually, he responded with many unreasonable questions and some feedback. My mentor was upset and wrote to the head of research because that committee member did not respond on time. She requested a replacement and refused to work with him. It worked in my favor. There are things that will happen, and sometimes we don't understand why, but God always has a way of working things out. His ways are not our ways.

The committee member was replaced with a lady, but not just any lady—a very humble lady. Again, things started going very well. I got my plan approved and started to write my actual dissertation manuscript. I wrote chapter one. For chapter two, the literature review, my school's request was to include 100 sources or references for this chapter. One night, as I sat up typing in the quiet of my home, I felt so discouraged. I felt like quitting, and I said to myself, Lord, why am I doing this to myself when I could be sleeping like everyone else? I am not doing this anymore; I quit.

I swung my executive chair around, and I turned on my television, which is always on 3 ABN (Angels Broadcasting Network). As soon as the television came on, I saw a Pastor saying, "You need to have faith and trust in God and His words," as he held up the Bible.

I turned off the television, swung my chair back around to my desk, and then smiled and said, "Lord, you knew I needed to hear this, thank you." I went right back to work and was able to complete not only the literature review, but the outline for chapters three, four, and five. God knows our need before we even ask, and He was on time with that message of hope for me. He will do the same for you.

Each quarter, we have to fill out a plan as to what we hope to achieve for that quarter. I filled out my plan stating that I wanted to achieve approval from my mentor, my committee members, and the school for my manuscript. The head of research wrote back and stated that I was too ambitious and not even my faith could allow me to get three approvals in one quarter. He wrote to my mentor and stated that I needed to change my plan. I felt discouraged because God was working on my behalf and now others were questioning my faith. I told my mentor that I was not changing my plan because I would be going against my faith and what I believed. I had already seen God's handy work. Why would I doubt that He is able?

My mentor said, "I would never ask you to go against your faith."

With that said, I gathered my data and completed and submitted my manuscript.

Lo and behold! I got more approvals than I had planned. I got mentor approval, committee approval, and school approval, and the dean signed off on my manuscript. My mentor organized my defense during the break. It is not the norm for committee members to agree to conduct the defense of my research during the break or time off from school, but my mentor was very helpful in convincing them. Everything went well, and I was congratulated and welcomed by my chair and committee members as "Dr. Ephraim." This was when reality struck me that I had achieved my blessing.

This journey helped me to grow spiritually and learn never to give up faith and trust in God, especially when He is already working in your favor. I stepped out in faith to pursue this career path, and it was God who brought me to it and through it. It was my prayer, hard work, determination, and dedication to God that made it all possible. I not only fulfilled my earthly father's dream for me, but I stayed rooted in my heavenly Father. God has done it for me, and He can do it for anyone who believes in Him and trusts Him. I challenge anyone to take that bold step in faith to fulfill whatever dream you are fearful to pursue. God will never leave you or forsake you. He will see you through. I do not have enough words in my mouth to praise Him. I will continue to serve Him and trust Him in everything I do because I have experienced firsthand how good my God is and that He is worthy to be praised. As the songwriter Ricardo Silva stated, "I would not take one step without Him, because I don't have the strength to make it on my own."

God Always Has a Way

Victor Olufemi

Unless we as human beings believe and key into the vast promises that God made to us, His believing children, we will continue to be limited. If you have ever started an activity, a project, or a program and have given up midway because you faced a challenge or difficulty, then I hope my testimony may challenge or motivate your faith.

I am a chartered accountant, and I am currently on my way to completing a doctoral program. As the fourth of six children, I had a humble beginning and faced challenges that affected my academic progress. No doubt, many people I met in life influenced my view of the world around me. Some people did not think I would amount to much in life, while others believed in me and encouraged me to strive for more in life. However, I desired to attain greater heights and believed that God had much more in store for me. Reading the word of God, trusting that His promises apply to me, and surrendering to His leading through the voice of His Spirit gave me direction and speed. I embraced the word of God in Proverbs 3:5-6 NIV: "Trust in the Lord with all your heart and lean not on your own understanding; in all your ways submit to him, and he will make your paths straight."

LEARNING TO ENTRUST MY CARES ON JESUS

I started working immediately after my secondary school education and became responsible for my needs without depending on anybody. Notwithstanding eking out a living at a young age, I had the dream to become a chartered accountant. My salary as an administrative clerk was barely enough to cover my living expenses, and I had no idea of how to finance and actualize the desire to continue my education. Yes, I was born into a Christian family, and I grew up with the understanding that the Lord answered prayers, but I had not learned how to surrender to Him, how to trust Him with the direction of my life, and how to listen to His voice for the desired leading.

When it comes to divine intervention, being a Christian by birth without having a personal encounter with Jesus limited my ability to entrust challenging situations completely to Him for resolution. I would always try to solve the problems instinctively despite having prayed for help. I kept on trying to do God's work for Him and encouraged myself with the scripture that faith without works was dead. I worked during the day, gave paid evening home lessons to the children of some of my superiors, and even taught local church choirs how to read staff notations just to make extra money. Earning legitimate income by being resourceful is not bad, but the problem with me then was that I trusted in my abilities and efforts to pave the way for my success instead of in God, who would make the seed of the efforts grow into a bountiful harvest. I prayed to God, but I did not fully entrust my dreams and challenges, my pains and my hopes, my life and expectations to Him.

Then one day, everything changed: I could not cope with the stress. I fell ill and landed in the hospital. There, when friends and family had gone home after visiting hours, the feeling of being all alone and tired became overwhelming. I told God that I did not want to fade out but instead manifest in the glory He had ordained for me. The prayer from my heart was for Jesus to help me solve all my problems so that I did not have to struggle, and He heard me. It took my lying helplessly and being lonely in the hospital to slow me down and realize that I had to let Jesus take over.

After being discharged from the hospital and resuming work, I became aware of vital information relevant to advancing my education but without the struggle. With Jesus in charge, I realized I had a surplus from my salary after meeting all my basic needs. I had stopped all the after-work lessons because of health reasons, but God still met my financial needs. I suddenly realized that I was enjoying the grace of God that I had not accessed before. The same tasks I did, which went unappreciated before, became the basis of my receiving monetary incentives.

I became friends with Ade, a staff member in the finance department where I worked. Prior to our becoming friends, we would pass each other by without my realizing that God was going to use him for me. He gave me the information about the Accounting Technician Scheme of the Institute of Chartered Accountants of Nigeria (ICAN) and assured me that my O-level result was relevant for enrollment. Ade also gave me the information about a lecture center that allowed installment payments of tuition fees. Where had this person with all the useful information been all along when I was struggling? All of a sudden, I had the information that made way for me, and I was on my way to achieving my dream.

You probably have been passing by your God-ordained destiny helper without realizing it. Surrender to God; tell Him to take over, and He will connect you to the divine helper He has arranged for you. He will open your ears and eyes to see that important piece that was there all the while, and which you need to solve your puzzle. According to 1 Peter 5:6-7 and verse 10, God wants you to submit yourself to Him so He may lift you up. Out of His love for you, He wants to take over all your worries so that you are free from suffering. God wishes to make you perfect, established, and strengthened. Let Him.

INSPIRATION TO MOVE HIGHER

As I continued working, the focus on my academic development was unwavering. God gave me great friends who encouraged and supported me with prayers and genuine companionship. The Holy Spirit prepared the heart of all the bosses I worked with in several units in the administration department. Even when I got a role change to the finance department to align with my desired career, God's favor never stopped. I became an associate accounting technician (AAT) and continued acquiring more qualifications as I gradually rose up the ranks to a position as a higher executive officer.

On the job, I got my Higher National Diploma (HND), became a chartered accountant, and still thirsted for more feathers in my cap. Before I proceeded with my HND, I met my wife to be, whom God used as an inspiration for me to keep moving higher. She was already a master's student, while I only had my AAT qualification, which was equivalent to an Ordinary National Diploma (OND). She believed in my future and stuck by me. When she hinted at enrolling for another master in public health, I was spurred to register for my master in business administration.

When you give God room to walk the journey of your life, His presence attracts the right people to you who will support you. According to Proverbs 13:20, walking with the wise inspires wisdom. Of course, the devil tries to counter God's actions by sending detractors. However, once you have learned to listen to the voice of God through His Spirit and yield to His leading, you can make the right choice to avoid unprofitable associations.

DOCTORAL JOURNEY: OVERCOMING A BARRIER TO PROGRESS

I embarked on the doctoral journey after I completed my MBA program, by which time I had left civil service for private sector employment and was doing very well financially. God had used my academic growth to get me established. When I started the first course in the doctoral program, I did not understand the flow of class discussions; everything sounded complex to me. The thought of not being able to cope with the high level of reasoning required for the course came into my heart. However, I remembered how, when I had run to Jesus with my problems in the past, He had answered me, and I became calm. My mother would always call on the Holy Spirit to help her in everything, even when I did not think that she should bother Him. I made a sincere plea to the Holy Spirit to help me. And true to John 14:27, the Holy Spirit gave me peace and gave me the reassurance that took away my fear.

For every discussion and assignment, I prayed before starting, and once I put my hands on the keyboard of my laptop, thoughts of what to write began to flow into my head. By the time I stopped typing to read what I had written down, I found that I had more than enough of the required word count. When I read my submission, I was often amazed at my advanced level of writing, and I even had a better understanding of the topic of discussion when I read what I had written.

As I progressed in the program, I became more confident but remained conscious of the fact that I always had help in the Holy Spirit. However, on several of the many days that my wife would critique my work, my ego gradually became inflated when she commented that my writings had reached a level that she could easily understand. Rather than acknowledge the source of my expanded knowledge, I reveled in the moment's glory and took much of the credit. Considering that I no longer struggled with responding to class discussions and completing assignments, I reduced the time I committed to praying before beginning my reading sessions and unconsciously relegated the Holy Spirit to the background, unlike when I had first started.

Then came a time when I had a major submission to make. I got ready to type and nothing came to my head; everything was blank. I convinced myself that I was simply exhausted from the day's work. The blankness for that particular assignment continued for a whole week, though I managed to submit routine discussions and responses. I realized there was a problem and quickly understood what the cause was. Pleading with the Holy Spirit to forgive my pride, I asked Jesus to advocate on my behalf.

I felt as if I had lost a super power. It is a terrible thing to lose the presence and support of the Holy Spirit.

I learned a practical lesson that pride is a terrible thing before the Lord. I understood that pride was a success destroyer and a requirement for falling from grace (Proverbs 16:18). The experience also made me understand James 4:6, that unless we humble ourselves before God, we cannot have grace activated. A danger even exists in not being able to identify or accept that pride has blocked off access to God's grace. Search yourself to see if this success killer has created a barrier between you and God. If indeed pride has gotten in the way, humble yourself before God and pray for mercy to get grace reactivated. God's love for me made me realize the barrier that could have hindered my progress or resulted in my failure. He made a way for me to move forward.

FINISHING WELL

I often hear the scripture quoted from Ecclesiastes 7:8 ESV that "better is the end of a thing than its beginning," but I better understood this while writing my doctoral study. Starting the doctoral journey was a significant step for me in the wake of the economic decline in Nigeria. I prayed before I started the program and trusted God to walk with me until its completion. As I continued, the first challenge was the ever-deteriorating exchange rate that negatively affected payment of tuition fees. However, because I had a well-paying job, I could combine paying my school fees with meeting family financial obligations.

God gave me the ease of coping with the rigors of the doctoral program, but challenges began to arise to prevent me from completing the good thing I had started. Opposition and prejudice occurred at work because of the fact that I had started the program. Some of my coworkers were not happy that I had started the program because it put me at an advantage over them. The apathy continued to the point that I had to resign my appointment, having tried everything I could to no avail so that I could finish with good grades. I had to choose between my job and the doctorate—my ticket to a wider horizon. If I had stayed on the job, I would have been frustrated to the point of not enjoying the work and not being able to perform well in the program.

At the point of being allocated dissertation committee members, my bank delayed the process of wiring my tuition fees, and I could not register on time for the semester. By the time I resolved the issue of being able to register, the three options of committee chair I selected were no longer available. Therefore, I got a committee chair who I knew nothing about, not knowing that God was working out His purpose for my rapid progress. I merely yielded to how He was running the affairs of my life. My testimony in that situation was that my friends who got chairs they opted for kept complaining that they were having relationship problems, while the God option for me was very competent and supportive. I was happy that God did not answer me according to the idols of my heart, which were the choices for committee chair that I had made earlier. God made the necessary arrangement for me to progress without any form of discouragement.

Working with God's choice of my committee chair, I advanced quickly and had my prospectus approved in no time. Within two dissertation classes, I had completed the draft of my proposal and entered the review stage. The school recommends five doctoral study classes to complete the program, and I am well ahead of the time frame to complete the journey. The pace of completion of the doctoral study depends on the individual student. As such, students in the class can be at different stages of doctoral study development. God has connected me with wonderful classmates, who are working at an advanced stage of their dissertation, and who inspire and motivate me to achieve accelerated progress. I have also given support to other classmates who are at the early stage of doctoral study development. The trials and testimonies of some of these classmates challenge my faith to become stronger. From all the interactions in both class and private communications, I have increased in knowledge beyond the doctoral study.

CONCLUSION

The pruning God has given my life gives me the assurance that no matter the situation or challenge ahead, all is well. I understand that the reason God wiped out the generation of the children of Israel who originally left Egypt in wilderness was because they refused to acknowledge God's ability to deliver despite the numerous mind blowing miracles He performed, which they had witnessed. My testimony does not end here because I am almost at the perfect ending of the doctoral journey. I have the assurance that I will finish well because the God who made a way before will make a way again. He always has a way!

Pursuing Excellence Without Excuse

Ranelli Williams

Soon after graduating with my MBA, I applied to the PhD program at Walden University and was accepted. However, being a person who went through college without loans—my mom paid for my undergraduate school and my employer paid for my MBA—the large loans that I would incur from the PhD program scared me, and I quickly withdrew my acceptance.

From time to time, the university would continue to send me information about their programs, and I had this nagging thought that this was something I wanted to pursue. In December 2010, I went on vacation to my home country, Montserrat, and upon my return to work, my director called me into her office.

"Ranelli," she said, "you have been with us for six years, and with your talent, you should at least be in a manager role, but there are just no such positions."

She went on to hand me a sheet of paper that contained a job posting for a manager role in another department. She said, "I think this role would be great for you. Take a look at it; if you are interested, I will reach out to the hiring manager on your behalf." At the time, I was an internal audit supervisor. The managerial position seemed like a great opportunity, so the process began for my application.

On my third day back to work, there was an emergency department meeting and we were told that due to restructuring, the department was being reduced from twenty to about six employees and they were co-sourcing the internal audit functions with one of the Big Four accounting firms. My position was one of the fourteen that would be eliminated.

I jumped into full gear to secure a position within my company because I was not ready to give up the tenure that I had established with them but also because my husband had recently lost his job a few months before. I was bold in my prayers and actions and not only landed that interview but also another interview for a separate manager position within my company.

In the meantime, I was advised to take the time to search for employment with full pay. I had a lot of time at home to seek God in the situation. One day, as I was scrolling the Internet, I landed on Tyler Perry's site. And although I do not remember the exact wording, I do remember that the message from God written on Tyler's page meant, "You can have it all." I told my cousin Marilyn that God said I could have it all based on the message I read on Tyler's page, and as I was talking to her, my phone rang. It was the HR department from my company offering me both jobs I had interviewed for. Both departments wanted me, so I had a choice. Look at God! I took a couple of days, made my choice, and continued with the same company without losing any of the benefits I had built up as a six-year employee.

In the meantime, Walden was still knocking, and I decided that this would be my way of securing a new career, should a similar situation happen in the future. And so, in March 2011, I became a doctor of business administration student at Walden University. Because I had completed my master's more than ten years prior, there were some management courses I was required to take. All was going well. I quickly completed the coursework required and moved into the doctoral study proposal phase, which is similar to the dissertation phase for PhDs. I chose my topic of study and began my research, and I worked on the two sections (chapters) needed for the proposal.

In 2012, I became pregnant with my second son. I was so determined not to skip a beat that although he was due in late December that year, I still enrolled for the November/December semester, hoping the semester would end before I gave birth. However, my son was born by C-section two weeks before his due date, and I still had one more week to complete the semester. I pushed through, worked while in the hospital, and finished up at home.

As a result of that hard push with a C-section and a new baby, I became burned out. I decided to take one semester off, which became two, three, and eventually four. Eight months had gone by without me working on my doctoral proposal. Once I returned after eight months, I just could not get my rhythm back. Working a part-time job, managing a household, and raising two small children, including a baby, became very difficult. Needless to say, that was a wasted semester for me. I hardly got anything accomplished. Feeling like a failure, I took the next semester off. Second bad move. I returned the following semester and repeated the cycle. I began getting more and more discouraged. There were times I contemplated quitting, but I would quickly remember former football player Vince Lombardi's words: "Winners never quit and quitters never win." For another year and a half, I edged forward, little by little.

While going through this slump, I recalled my cousin, Akiah Powell, who suddenly passed away in 2012 at the age of twenty-one, three months before graduating college. She was scheduled to attend law school that fall. Her school said this about her: "Akiah epitomized our program's slogan: 'Pursuing Excellence Without Excuse.' She was certainly more than a student, she was a scholar!" As I contemplated those words and my younger cousin's legacy, I knew I had to push harder. I knew I had to focus on pursuing excellence without excuse. No matter what was going on in my life, I had to finish what I had started and finish strong.

In September 2016, I decided to attend a writing intensive in Baltimore, Maryland. That changed things for me. I knew it was time to really buckle down and get this done. At that writing intensive, I accomplished in three and a half days what I had not accomplished in three and a half years. All it takes is the will to win, the right surroundings, and the right support, and so much can be accomplished. I came back home, determined to get this done in 2017. With that resolve, God already had my support system lined up. When I returned to class in November, I was paired with a buddy who was exactly what I needed in an accountability partner. He pushed me, requested deadlines for me to have sections done, offered feedback on my work, and was just a wonderful support to me.

Don't think life did not get in the way again because it certainly did. I was the co-host for a conference in November of

2016, which was much more demanding on my time than I had expected. The day of the conference, I learned my uncle passed suddenly of a heart attack and my family had to travel to Europe for the funeral. Right before we left, we got the news that my husband had prostate cancer, another devastating blow with its unique challenges and decisions. Then there was the 2017 tax season and teaching at the community college during the spring semester that competed for my time. To top it off, in March 2017, one month after we found out about my aunt's cancer diagnosis, she passed away. As I dealt with all this, I thought, *do I stop or do I keep going to finish what I started?*

My answer was to finish what I had started. Akiah's last words on her Facebook page were, "I can do all things through Christ who strengthens me." I hold this scripture from Philippians 4:13 close to my heart as I continue this journey. At the time of this writing, I have completed my proposal and expect to have it approved by the time this book is published. My goal is to continue to pursue excellence without excuse and be Dr. Ranelli Williams by early fall of 2017.

My message to you is exactly what the title of this chapter says: "Pursue excellence without excuse." This can be applied to any area of your life. Regardless of what you are called to do, your responsibility is to eliminate the excuses and run with excellence, knowing that all things are possible with God.

COURAGEOUS ADVENTURES

Six Faith Walkers Share Their Defeat
Over Various Life's Challenges

I Will Never Leave You

Elizabeth Lindsey

I was born and raised on the island of Montserrat in the West Indies where I was educated and started my career as a nurse. During the time I worked in Montserrat, I learned to be an advocate for both my patients and coworkers. My parents, Matthew and Henrietta Lindsey, believed the Bible and taught their children to have faith and trust in God. I grew up believing the words of the Bible, but one verse that has stood out is Philippians 4:13 BSB, "I can do all things through Christ who gives me strength." The path to faith and belief is not always smooth, but trusting God and His many promises strengthened my faith. Jeremiah 32:27 KJV states, "Behold, I am the Lord, the God of all flesh: is there any thing too hard for me?" It was David's belief in God that helped him to be victorious over the giant Goliath. If God was there for David, I know He will be there for me and for you also.

A Journey Through Faith

A journey is the act of traveling from one place to another. There are many traffic signs posted on the journey to any destination, but the destination must be decided before seeking directions. Sometimes after seeking directions the unexpected happens, but one must be ready to take a detour and recalculate the route. Posted signs include roadblocks and detours, which occurred very early on in my journey of life. My initial career destination was to be a teacher, and I set out to follow that path, but I was put on the teacher's waiting list and grew tired of being unoccupied and unemployed.

I was then encouraged to join the nursing profession, but I was not interested in becoming a nurse because I did not like many processes involved. After some thought, I did decide to join the profession because the thought of being unemployed versus being temporary employed, even in a field I was not very interested in, gave me the inclination to try the latter on a temporary basis. I went through the required processes, was accepted into the field of nursing, and started out with the plan I had in mind, which was to go along with the nursing program to completion or until I was called to the teaching profession, which was the career of my choice. But when I was called to teach, I was no longer interested, so I continued through the three years needed to complete general nursing and the one year to complete the midwifery program.

By that time, I no longer had an aversion for nursing; I had a new community of friends and was excited in my newfound career. I continued working as a nurse for years before accepting the challenge to become a nurse anesthetist. The overwhelming thought of being a teacher was no longer prominent in my mind. I left Montserrat to complete the nurse anesthetist program on another island and returned to work in that capacity on completion of the program. I felt gratified and enjoyed my new career along with the financial benefits.

On my return to the island, much of my family, friends, and colleagues had relocated. When I encountered them during visits, they would try to convince me to relocate, constantly reminding me that I was the only one left from our group, and giving me reasons why I should relocate. I missed being with them, but I enjoyed being at home and giving service to my local islanders. I felt that my contribution in my native island was invaluable. In retrospect, my initial career choice of teaching was not the path that God wanted for me, and my decision to stay in Montserrat was not God's plan either. God does not compel anyone to go against his or her will but makes them willing to follow even if He has to change some situations.

A Change of Plans

When my daughter completed her secondary education, which is equivalent to high school in the United States, she wanted to continue her studies, but this was not an option for her on the island. I was gainfully employed and therefore was not interested in college education at that time. And because a college education was not available on the tiny island, it was a plan that seemed out of reach. However, I knew the importance of a higher education and I wanted this for her too. Several thoughts went through my mind regarding my next detour and the journey needed to reach the desired destination. I accept as true the last portion of Matthew 6:3 that says "do not let the right hand know what the left is doing," if and when it pertains to my personal decisions.

This storytelling is out of character for me, and I do not want to pontificate my own accolades, but I think that sharing my story can help someone realize that if we allow God to lead, He will do more for us than we are able to ask, think, or desire. I was not prepared for the changes that I would need to make, so I prayed for guidance. My faith in God got me through because I could not see where this detour was taking me, but one after another, things fell into place.

The idea of relocating to the United States became prominent because my sister lived in New York, and I knew that was one avenue I could explore. I ventured out to research possibilities and the necessary steps that I needed to take while trying to sort out my direction. At that time, one requirement for foreign nursing graduates to work in the United States was to take the certificate for graduate foreign nursing schools (CGFNS) exam prior to the licensing (NCLEX) exam. I took the exam, and while awaiting the results, I was offered a promotion, which required leaving the island in September to pursue a course that would enhance my new position. I scheduled vacation in July for two months but was called to complete the necessary paperwork for the program I was expected to attend on my return from vacation. There were detours, roadblocks, accidents, fog, and other problems that prevented the smooth flow of traffic, and although I wavered at times, my faith held strong.

As I contemplated what to do next, I called upon God for help in choosing the best path that would be most beneficial and rewarding for my family and me. I told God that I would accept the first clear path as the Go sign from Him. That week, I received the result of my CGFNS exam with a passing score. I knew then that was what God wanted me to do. Just before leaving for vacation, I was again approached by a trusted friend who tried to dissuade me from leaving, pointing out the possibilities and benefits of my new position. It was then when I heard a voice within saying, "Go forward. I will be with you and will fight for you."

Romans 12:3 tells us that God has given to every man a measure of faith. We all may have different measures of faith, but utilizing that faith according to that which we have is very important. The Bible states in Matthew 13:31-32 KJV "the kingdom of heaven is like to a grain of mustard seed, which a man took and sowed in his field: Which indeed is the least of all seeds: but when it is grown, it is the greatest among herbs, and becometh a tree, so that the birds of the air come and lodge in the branches thereof." In Matthew 17:20, the Bible also notes that if we have faith as little as a mustard seed, we can command the mountain to move and it will. What I understand here is that faith can be expanded when the right circumstances exist. The faith and trust that I had and still have in God gave me that confidence to boldly move forward. I reached out to my sister and soon left to join her in the United States. I trusted God and I was determined to move forward on this new journey—my bold move. I cannot say that my move was all smooth sailing, but as long as God is in the ship, we can always smile at any storm.

My Final Destination

I made that bold move because of my belief in God, and I left with the faith that God would help me work through any situation. Once in the United States, with all my paperwork in hand, I walked into the closest hospital in the area where my sister lived to speak with the recruiter, even though I didn't have an appointment. The recruiter was very pleasant and accommodating. After that initial encounter and interview, I knew that God had led me there and He had handled all the transactions. The needed processes were in motion. I was told to ask my sister not to attempt to make a petition on my behalf to change my work status because of the duration of time it would take to complete the process. I was advised to allow the company to process the paperwork, which would expedite and shorten my waiting time. It took about three months for me to get a working visa and get a graduate nurse permit to work at the facility until I passed the state board (NCLEX) exam and became a registered nurse. I was very excited about how the sequence of events fell into place and started the process to write the state board exam on the next available date.

My first day on the job was November 28, and I signed up to take the state board in February of the following year. My friends who previously took the NCLEX told me that it was not a good idea to take the state board within such a short period of time since I was unfamiliar with the American system. I thought about it but did not change my date because I knew that God was leading the way. While I was waiting for the state board exam, I was encouraged to attend review classes, but I completed the reviews on my own. Between November 28 and when I took the exam in February, all my leisure time was spent reading and reviewing.

Thank God I passed the state board in one sitting that February. On the first day of the exam, I felt fine and everything went well. On the second day, I woke up feeling miserable and with a fever of 103°F. My sister advised me to call and cancel the exam for that day because I was not feeling well, but I did not know what effect the cancellation would have, so I made the attempt anyway. I really felt horrible that day. I slept in the exam room on the desk for short periods during the exam, but I was successful. God helps those who help themselves.

I will not pretend that everything went as smoothly as I would have loved it to. About the time the exam results should have been available to me, my head nurse kept asking me if I had received my results, which made me a little nervous because I was aware that other test takers had already received their results. Many days I cried at work and on my way home, but I made sure no one saw me cry except for God. Eventually, I received a letter from the state education department indicating that there were discrepancies in my paperwork, which were very easy for me to correct. My birthdate is April 26, I took my general nursing exam on April 25 and my midwifery exam on April 27, and for some reason they interchanged the dates. I had my birth certificate and my diplomas on hand, which I forwarded to them to clarify the discrepancies. I eventually received a congratulatory letter stating that I had passed the state board and that my diploma would follow.

My big blessings continued. I went on to pursue my bachelor in nursing, master in healthcare administration and am now pursuing the doctor of nursing program. My daughter, whose request to attend college forced me to leave my comfort zone and move to the United States, has completed her bachelor's degree, master's degree, and is almost finished with her doctorate. I have also fulfilled my love for teaching by being a clinical instructor in the hospital and an adjunct professor at private and community colleges. I am blessed to witness nursing students graduate and move on to take their places in the profession, some of them working alongside me at the same institution. My motto now includes the words of the song by Mahalia Jackson: "If I can help somebody as I really ought, then my living shall not be in vain, therefore I am determined to do all that is within my capacity to assist my fellow men and women to achieve their dreams."

THE FAITH WALKER'S JOURNEY

Hebrews 11 gives us a complete synopsis of what faith is and how we can manifest our faith. The start and end point must be carefully mapped out before we leave on any journey. The Bible is our guide for direction and destination. Have faith and trust God.

On our journey, traffic problems sometimes appear so large and frequently that they overwhelm us. We should never get discouraged or fearful, but like David, fight in the name of the Lord Jesus, who promised that "he will never leave or forsake us." I close this chapter with the words from Isaiah 41:10, 13, 18, and 20: "Fear thou not; for I am with thee: be not dismayed; for I am thy God: I will strengthen thee; yea, I will help thee...yea, I will uphold thee with the right hand of my righteousness. For I the Lord thy God will hold thy right hand, saying unto thee, Fear not; I will help thee. I will open rivers in high places, and fountains in the midst of the valleys: I will make the wilderness a pool of water, and the dry land springs of water."

This story tells just a portion of my big blessings, and I hope it has achieved the goal of the book, which is "to teach men and women to follow and trust God's instructions." I would rather say it is to *inspire* men and women to follow and trust God's instructions. May this chapter be a blessing to all its readers. Take courage in the promises of God, for He never goes back on His word.

A Story of Faith, Perseverance, and Self-Worth

La'Shonda DeBrew

I am La'Shonda DeBrew and my mission is to empower and inspire women who desire to be financially independent to not let anything stop you from realizing your dreams and becoming all that He has purposed you to be! Significant events that shaped who I am today and gave me the determination to succeed are etched in my memory as early as third grade. Even though I may have been too young to understand the practical applications of the Bible, I was taught at a very young age in church and Sunday school about the power of the word, prayer, faith, and who I was in Him! Many strong influential women around me, namely my mother and aunts, instilled in me and nurtured my self-worth.

I would daydream all of the time about what my life would be like when I was old enough to make decisions and be in control of my destiny. I'm talking about reaching that point in your life beyond high school where you become accountable and responsible and in the driver's seat, living out your life according to who God says you are and not living based on your circumstances of what you've come through or what you're going through. There were many uphill battles, but my focus was on the outcome and what I had to accomplish. When I focused this way, it was easier to achieve goals and not let the walls close around me. *You will find that the walls will close in if you take your eyes off of the goal and vision of the accomplishment.*

My mother was a teacher and took care of her household as a single parent. In order to make ends meet, she had many other "hustles" that we are all familiar with, such as selling Tupperware and ceramics, cooking, and baking. For a time in between, when she was riffed from her job, she was also a babysitter. I didn't want for anything and as far as I was concerned, all needs were taken care of. We always had plenty of everything; I couldn't ask for anything more. Thinking about how she persevered under those circumstances, I was inspired and even more determined to do whatever I set my mind to.

Throughout my high school years, I worked various summer jobs, including a position in the Mayor's Youth Leadership program. I was grateful for the opportunities, and they confirmed that I needed to keep it moving and pursue my goal of attending college. I was not prepared nor ready to start that work life! So when it was time, I proceeded to apply for acceptance to college. Upon high school graduation, I set out on my mission of going away to North Carolina A&T State University. My first semester, there were no rooms available, so I had to return home and try again the next semester. I decided to stay in North Carolina with my father and grandparents because it was closer and I was determined to get into college and not go back home.

After a semester layover, I was finally in school, but I needed to figure out how I would pay tuition. I used a combination of the Pell Grant, financial aid, and student loans and did that every semester for three semesters before I finally came to the realization that building up student loan debt and figuring out payment for every semester, along with not having any money for other expenses, was not the way to go. Reluctantly, I left to go back home to finish school in-state and work a full-time job in order to have income for living expenses.

For me, getting a college education was the priority and non-negotiable. I continuously prayed and sought out ways to make it happen. The help came in the form of job tuition assistance for classes and participating in leadership programs, which supported upward mobility and included college classes that were related to my current position. It took me longer to finish since I was working and going to school, but I didn't stop going to school. I was focused on the accomplishment and the vision. Things would happen along the way and although I attended three different schools, I finally graduated with a bachelor's degree. The last sixty credits of my degree were actually completed in an eighteen-month accelerated program where I attended class all day on Saturdays—yes, it was eight hours.

I was married, my son was nine months old, and I was working a full-time job. The main challenge here was completing the thesis assignments that were due every six weeks at the end of a class. I also completed several leadership programs while I attended college in pursuit of more opportunities that offered a promotion and more money. As a young adult, I would think about what career to choose that would make enough money so that I was able to support my household, provide for my family, and be financially independent. I definitely wanted to meet all of my needs and all, if not most, of my wants. And I was able to do that and make that dream come true as I got closer and closer to finishing the degree program.

With God, anything is possible. He continued to show me that being ready and not always "getting ready" places you in a position with options to explore. Having options was something that was important to me because, growing up, the majority of the households in my family were financially dependent on the women. The message that I received from this dynamic was that as women, we should always know our worth and value and be in a position to support ourselves or households no matter what.

With this mindset, although I was married and we had two incomes, I was always on a mission to learn about and put the items in place that would create financial stability for myself and family. I started my career as a clerk typist and continued to receive promotions and move up. I began studying ways to increase your wealth and eventually participated in real estate investment opportunities, started an investment club, and purchased a franchise business. Throughout it all, I thank the Lord for the accomplishments, peaks and valleys, lessons learned, mistakes, and failures. I often pondered quitting or stepping back, but then I asked myself, where would I be had I not taken the chance? And the answer is that I would've been in the same place as where I started. I would not know what I know now and I would not be where I am if I had not kept it moving without looking back. It was definitely a walk of faith and perseverance.

When you are on a journey, all of your accomplishments—no matter how small—fit into your BIG goal of taking the limits off and having what He says you can have, so trust that He will provide what you need. It's not easy, but it can be done if you don't look at what you can't do but instead at what you can do.

There was some researching in order to know where my husband and I needed to start and who to go to, but a lot was figured out as we went along. We adjusted the plan as needed to fit the goals. I became a student of finance and researched whatever we needed to know in order to support the vision. We planned and tracked as we accomplished milestones along the way. You may think that setting goals of achieving something greater and bigger than you is hard, but just existing and not living can be hard all by itself because you limit your resources and never grow or know what you are capable of, including experiencing all that life has to offer. It's a matter of perspective. Back then, I didn't see it as being hard because to me, being broke was hard; not having anything was hard. It was also easier mentally to work on achieving my goals because I had never failed at this; it was all new to me. When we have preconceived notions and failures, our judgment is clouded and we are tricked into thinking that it can't be done. That's not true! If you did it before, you can definitely do it again; and if you started from ground zero before with no experience in that area, why can't you do it again when you know more now than you did before?

There were many lessons learned during these seasons and times of my life. It is He who allows us to do what we do and be successful at what we do. It's easy to think that we are in control and responsible for where we are because "we've" worked to get there, but without Him, there would be no *me*! Without his presence, grace, and mercy, I don't know where I'd be. At one point, I thought that it was me making money and that I was in control. But things started happening that I had no control over and could not resolve with money due to lack of it or circumstances beyond my control. I could no longer throw money at the problem, and I realized that these were problems that could not be resolved with money, no matter how much you had in the bank. When a devastating event occurs, it attacks your self-confidence, self-assurance, self-worth, and honestly, it challenges your faith! Without money to solve it, you are forced to throw your hands up and watch God work. You have to exercise your faith and pray about how to proceed. You must tap back into and recognize your worth, which has nothing to do with the amount of money in your checking account. Wealth comes from the inside out, not the outside in. You can have money but not feel worthy or wealthy and operate with a poor mindset.

When you are paralyzed, stuck, and in your head, mental blocks will stop you from moving forward until they are released. The mental blocks can be fear that has set in, which makes you confused and constantly feeling panicked. You may play the story over and over in your mind. You don't know who you are anymore. You are more focused on what you don't have. I've learned from experience that in order to clear these blocks, when you are going through an attack on your finances or you are rebuilding from a financial setback, it's imperative that you get still, focus, meditate, pray, fast, use daily affirmations and clear away negativity. Reserve a day to get clear. Recognize that you are your most valuable asset. Count your blessings and list them one by one! Complete a knowledge and skills assessment. Generate revenue based on the fastest path to cash now. Focus on just one thing to execute now. It's great to also talk to someone who can relate with what you're going through and support you as you are restoring financial peace. Ask yourself what you truly believe because that makes all of the difference in you moving forward toward financial independence.

"Whatever the mind can conceive and believe,
it can achieve."

—Napoleon Hill

The Healing Hand of God

Kim Jones

It was 1999. I was a bank supervisor in a fast-paced call center. It wasn't my dream job, but I had a paycheck. I always wanted to be an entrepreneur. I wanted to use my voice to speak to and empower women to do more and be more. I wanted to be known as Kim Jones, a world-renowned motivational speaker and bestselling author. Although I never fell in love with working for someone else, I was never surrounded by people who owned their own businesses, so my mindset was to work and have good benefits. However, I would think of witty ideas and ways to make money every waking moment. I knew I could have more, but the one thing I knew was that the "more" did not involve being stuck in that call center. I hated working all different shifts because someone else told me I had to do it.

I talked to customers eight hours a day, Monday through Friday, but I wanted to use my voice in a different way. I visualized myself in a large arena speaking to women. I used to practice speaking in the mirror as if I were in front of thousands. One day, as I was speaking with a customer, my throat was becoming sore, but I didn't pay much attention to it because growing up as a child, I always suffered from tonsillitis. My mother would take me to the doctor, who would prescribe penicillin for two weeks, after which I'd be fine.

This went on for many years into my early adulthood, so when my throat began to hurt, I didn't think anything strange about it. As the days went on, the soreness in my throat was gone, but laryngitis set in. After a week with laryngitis, I went to the doctor who told me I had allergies. I thought that to be very strange because I had never suffered from allergies before. I figured he knew best because he was the doctor. I didn't question what he said. I took the medication he gave me in hopes that it was just allergies and that soon I would be my old self again. But after a week, I still felt the same. It was not doing anything for me. I wasn't in any pain at all; I just had a touch of laryngitis. I went back to the doctor and he told me to have patience, that my body was not reacting to the medication, so he prescribed another medication. I believed him so I went home with the new medication and began to take it in hopes that it would work.

As the days went by, my voice got worse. Once, my daughter Cymone was downstairs, and I was trying to call her, but only a whisper came out. I could make a sound with some words, but with other words, there was no sound at all. It began to hurt to whisper because I was putting all my strength in trying to get the words out. I was literally banging on the walls in my house to call out to her. I was going to work every day, but trying to speak or even whisper was painful. Again, I found myself at the doctor telling him that something was seriously wrong.

He stated to me, and I quote, "Sister girl, you are fine."

He kept telling me to just trust him—my voice would come back. He really tried to convince me that I had allergies and nothing more. My boss told me to get a second opinion because clearly something was wrong. The medication should not make me worse by any means. I was given three different medications and still couldn't get out a full sentence. As the days went by, the whispers became silence. There were no words to be heard out of my mouth. I then made an appointment to get a second opinion. A good friend of mine recommended an ear, nose, and throat (ENT) specialist. I made the appointment with the hope that something would be found other than allergies.

The day of my appointment, I still had no voice, so I had to do some fancy mouthing to the receptionist. I was told to have a seat until the doctor called me into his office. I had no idea what was about to happen. Finally, the doctor called me in and told me to take a seat on the table. He asked me why I was there. I did the best I could to communicate to him what was going on with me. The ENT doctor didn't agree with my primary doctor that it was allergies so he decided to do a laryngoscopy. This is a visual examination below the back of the throat, where the voice box (larynx) containing the vocal cords is located. This was all new to me, and fear began to set in.

The doctor took the medical device and inserted it up my nose and down my throat to see exactly what was going on with my voice. I could feel him moving the device around in my throat looking for the cause. After a few minutes of looking, he removed the device, took a deep breath, and gave me the news.

He said, "Well, Mrs. Jones, you don't have allergies for sure. You have a polyp sitting right in the middle of your vocal cords."

My heart didn't drop because I wasn't sure what that meant. So I mouthed, "What does that mean to me? Will I get my voice back? Will I ever speak again? What?"

He told me that when we breathe, the vocal cords spread apart so that air can pass into and out of the lungs. But when we speak, the cords come together, causing the air from the lungs to pass through a smaller space. This causes the vocal cords to vibrate. The sound from these vibrations goes up the throat and comes out of the mouth as a person's voice. However, the polyp sat right in the middle, so my cords were not coming together, which was the reason no sound was being made.

My heart began to beat a little faster as he continued to talk. So many things were running through my mind. I asked him what could be done to remove the polyp and how I could get my voice back. He stated surgery was the only way.

If anyone knows me, they know that I don't like surgery in any way, shape, or form. I don't even like anesthesia. I have three kids who were all born through natural birth with no oral medication because I don't like to take medication. He told me that the surgery was not an easy surgery and there were side effects, one of which was that the vocal cord could potentially be cut during the procedure. Wait—did he just say "cut"? He then proceeded to tell me that during the surgery, there was a chance of my front teeth being knocked out by the instrument they would be using. This could not be happening right now. I was so lost in that moment. I had never had that feeling before in my life, and the story doesn't end there. I was told the polyp could be cancerous so I would have to make a decision as soon as possible!

The room was spinning. I could see the words coming out of his mouth, but I could no longer hear what he was saying. This man standing here in front of me was saying that the polyp he just saw on my vocal cords could be cancerous and that he could remove the polyp but could cut my vocal cords, preventing me from speaking again.

I thought, how do I process all this information? How do I digest this? It was too much to take in. I couldn't hear another word he said. He wanted me to make an appointment right away for the surgery, and I just was not ready for that. We went back and forth about scheduling an appointment and I told him I wanted to wait to see what would happen. Against his will, he agreed to give me a couple of weeks to come back and recheck the polyp to see if it shrank in any way.

When I left the office, my hands were shaking as I tried to hold on to the steering wheel. All I could do was say, Lord, help me. God, I can't do this one by myself. The enemy is trying to strip me of my voice. He is trying to take away my say in the world. The voice that I use to praise the Lord, the voice that I use to encourage my daughter and tell her I love her every day. The voice that said "I do" to my husband. Lord, you have to help me get my voice back.

"I will bless the Lord at all times: his praise shall continually be in my mouth."

—Psalms 34:1 KJV

As I was crying out, I realized I had to pull it together. I had to get my prayer warriors in place because we had to bombard heaven on my behalf. This was not my destiny; this was not the course set for my life. I had too much to live for and too much to give to the world. I had too much to say. The enemy wasn't going to silence me.

I was in a women's ministry that met every Tuesday evening. I also had a sister friend Gloria and she could definitely get a prayer through. So what was I afraid of? Why did I fear this thing? I began to call on my prayer warriors and we went into prayer and fasting. I began to listen to healing scriptures in my car every day. Gloria and I went to a natural healing store and read up on polyps. A book stated to take 2000 mg of vitamin C every day, so that's exactly what I did—because we still have to do what is required in the natural.

A couple of weeks passed, and I still could not speak, so I went back to the doctor and he checked it again. He stated that the polyp did shrink a little but not enough to make a difference. He still wanted me to get the surgery. I was still at a place where I was truly against having the surgery. I could remember Gloria telling me not to sign up for the surgery and that I needed to trust God. That kept ringing in my mind, and I would not sign up for the surgery. He told me that if he saw a hundred women in my age group, he would advise the surgery because of the chance of it being cancer. But I couldn't do it. I could not sign the papers. I knew God was a healer and this was a small thing to Him. I had to take a bold stand. I was standing firm on His word: "The LORD protects and preserves them—they are counted among the blessed in the land—he does not give them over to the desire of their foes. The LORD sustains them on their sickbed and restores them from their bed of illness" (Psalms 41:2-3 NIV).

My doctor said he wanted to see me again on January 3, 2000, to sign the papers for the surgery. By that time, he was getting antsy and really wanted me to make a decision.

Then one night at the women's ministry, we were told to write down exactly what it was we wanted from God. As the women were writing out their prayers, I thought carefully about what I wanted to write down. I began writing down exactly what I wanted God to do for me. I wrote on the paper, "On January 3, 2000, I go back to the doctor. I want this polyp to be completely gone." It was plain, simple, and to the point. This is what I wanted God to do. We put the prayers in an envelope and put them on the floor and prayed over them. We let our request be known unto God. I believed that it was already done. I was taking a bold move to trust God and not get the surgery.

So the day had come. January 3 was here. This was the day to show that doctor the God I serve is bigger than the surgery. I arrived at the doctor still without a voice. As I entered the room and sat on the table, he said to me, "Well, here goes." He took the device and put it up my nose and down my throat. He was moving the device around my throat to the point I was gagging, but he kept moving it around. When he finally removed the device, he looked at me in disbelief and said, "It is *completely gone.*"

I looked at him and nearly jumped off the table. That was my prayer. I prayed that this polyp would be completely gone. I knew it was God; I knew He had healed me. The doctor said there wasn't even a scar on my vocal cords to suggest a polyp was even there. I had stood on God's word and believed in His healing power. I knew that my voice would be used to empower.

My voice didn't come back right away, but one day, it finally did. I have learned through this that if you just stand boldly on God's word that it will not come back void. Know that God is a healer and take a bold leap of faith in your life and let God show Himself mighty. No matter what it looks like, God has the last say. Today, I use this same voice that the enemy tried to take from me to *speak* and empower women to do more and to be more. To God be the glory!

From Broke to Better

Dee Edwards

Did you have this idea that you were going to create a better life for yourself than the one you are living right now? Maybe you said that you were going to provide a better life for your children, better manage your money, obtain a higher credit score, get out of debt, or marry the person of your dreams and live happily ever after? Then, all of a sudden, real life hit you. You quickly realized that what you desired, the picture-perfect life that you couldn't wait to live, may only be a dream.

Over a decade ago, I found myself being the person I dreaded. I had over twenty credit cards, title loans, no family support, no job, and to top it off, I was mentally drained. I felt like I was in this world all by myself. I was a functioning social depressant. I knew how to make everyone around me feel good, but I was on the verge of a mental breakdown. People only saw my smile and laughter. The truth is, I was doing just about everything to keep from falling apart. I was masking my internal pain. All the odds were against me, and I was fighting to climb out of the hole I dug for myself. I was crying out for help, but no one was listening. I was screaming, but there was no sound. I was in desperate need of help and no one seemed to understand that I was on the verge of throwing in the towel. I almost gave up.

Have you ever felt like that or made one of these statements?

- This can't happen for me.

- This is all I deserve.

- I'll never get ahead.

- Nothing good happens to me.

- I'll never get married.

- Nobody loves me.

- I don't need friends.

- I'm ugly.

- I'm too fat.

- She's better than me.

- I hate myself.

- Why is this happening to me?

- I'm a failure.

- I might as well not try.

- I'm not smart enough.

- I can't do it.

- There's no way out.

If you have these poverty thoughts or similar words repeating themselves like a broken record in your mind, these thoughts and words have become your belief. They have become your voice. Every time you try to step outside the box or do something that you've always wanted to do, such as lose weight, change your spending habits, apply for a new job or promotion, save money, or start dating, nothing changes because of your belief system. Negative words and thought patterns have become the stones that are building the house in which you are living in today. However, you have the power to tear down these walls and barricades that are interfering with your ability to achieve your ultimate goal.

Now the real question is: how did you get here? How did you allow life's disappointments, heartaches, setbacks, and—let's be honest—decisions to leave you feeling so broken, dejected, and downcast? When did you stop progressing? When did you move out of the way and allow other people to start living your dreams? What happened to you? Look around—this isn't your life. You were created to live a purposeful life. A life filled with meaning, abundance, love, joy, and peace. However, you have been blindly walking through life with the entire world on your shoulders. You've been carrying everyone's burden and neglecting you.

Once, my counselor, Verrick Taylor, helped me to understand that my needs are important too and that I had to stop trying to become the solutions to everyone's problems. I shifted my focus and started putting me first. Originally, I thought I was the cause for every bad thing that happened in my life, but then I realized that bad things happen to good people with an intent for us to become *better* people. James 1:2-4 NLT says, "When troubles of any kind come your way, consider it an opportunity for great joy. For you know that when your faith is tested, your endurance has a chance to grow. So let it grow, for when your endurance is fully developed, you will be perfect and complete needing nothing."

Therefore, when you are going through situations of any kind, whether you're faced with bad news, failing health, ruined marriage, financial shortfalls, or lack of faith, your endurance—your ability or strength to continue or last despite fatigue, stress, or other adverse condition—your stamina is increasing. It's growing. That's why what you have been through hasn't killed you. That's why you push when you feel like giving up. Your endurance is growing, so let it mature. Become fully developed so you will be complete and perfect, lacking nothing.

In real life, we all have something to complain about. We've all done things we've regretted, but none of those things should interfere with God's plan for our life. But like me, many of us don't realize that our choices and mistakes don't change what's destined for us; our mindset does. It can redirect the course of our life negatively or positively. We have put ourselves in a box that was initially built out of paper, that could have been torn down easily with one blow. Now it has become a brick room with no windows, no doors, and no escape. You feel trapped.

But there is a way out. Initially, we don't see it because we are looking through the eyes of trauma and setback. It's time to look again—this time with a new perspective and a changed mindset. Although I felt entrapped in my situation and circumstances, there was something inside of me that was nudging me to step out on faith, but fear had a grip on my life. I was in a tug of war: should I stay in the same place or should I move forward?

I can't explain it, but I knew I was created for a greater purpose. Every day you blame yourself for your choices or decide not to move forward, your thought patterns are affirming every negative word that you believe about you. You are silencing the giant in you and listening to the words around you. Those words become your truth that keep you in a broken state of mind that continues to keep you stuck until struggling becomes the story of your life. Being broke is going through life as if you are just surviving with no purpose. Almost as if you have given up on being better. Being broke is not about money. Being broke is a mindset that weighs and influences your money, relationships, health, and well-being. But you can change that by changing your thought patterns.

You have to first believe that the Lord has a plan for you. According to Jeremiah 29:11, "They are plans for good and not for disaster, to give you a future and a hope." What do you believe about your life? Do you believe that you can come out? You may not know how your situation can change, but if you are going to transition from broke to better, you have to first understand that good things are awaiting you. That God can truly restore your life. But if you think that nothing good can happen to you or for you, it won't. I once read in Proverbs 23:7 KJV that as a man "thinketh in his heart, so is he." Whatever you think, you become. You can move to a nicer neighborhood, drive expensive cars, and make all the money in the world, but if your mindset is impoverished, then all the material gain will not last nor satisfy the inner desire for greater. Your mindset must change.

Most of us carry our learned beliefs and behaviors into adulthood until we learn differently and become exposed to a better way of thinking. It took me a long time to realize that I could have more. But my broke mindset told me that God didn't love me, and I was the only one going through troubles and trials. I just wished and prayed that I could make $9.00 an hour, have a better job, live in a nice apartment, and have a car note—my ideal life. But when I learned that creating my world started with my thinking, I began to dream bigger. I began to believe that I was worth more than $9.00 an hour, I could own my own car and house, and slowly, things in my life started to shift.

The transition to thinking and believing differently wasn't easy because thinking positively about myself and about my life wasn't natural for me. I had to make it a habit to think and speak positively over my situations, no matter the outcome. Now, if those old thoughts come up, I quickly retract my statement and pull down every negative word that is contrary to my new mindset and release positive affirmations into the atmosphere. And when I feel myself reverting back to the old me, I check my surroundings. Who have I been connected to? What have I been listening to? What is my environment feeding me? The key to developing and maintaining a positive mindset and shift from broke to better is being surrounded by people who also share the same way of thinking as you do.

I used to think that I was in control of the decisions that I made, regardless of the environment I was in, which, you can be, but if you are constantly in negative conditions or surrounded by people whose mindsets are conflicting with your new thought process, you are subconsciously planting those seeds into the back of your mind. And at the most vulnerable times, you will find yourself acting and thinking like the people who you thought were not influencing your mindset.

According to 1 Corinthians 15:33 NIV, "Do not be misled: Bad company corrupts good character." The company you keep should be of people who are positive, uplifting, and who desire success and more out of life. Like-minded individuals. Growing up, people always considered me the good girl—smart, loving, funny, and kind—but the company I kept gave me the reputation of a hard core, thuggish, heartless individual.

I was once introduced to a girl who would "boost" (steal) clothes from department stores and then sell them for more than half off the retail price. Well, one day, I went to the store with her only to show her what I wanted her to steal for me. I watched her and said to myself that if she could do it, I could do it too. I stole my first shirt. Never in a million years had I ever thought about stealing anything, but the company—not her influence, but being in her presence—changed my convictions. She never persuaded me; she never asked me; as a matter of fact, she didn't even agree with my decision. I learned early on that "birds of a feather flock together" is a true statement. There's something deep rooted in us that causes us to want to be around individuals who don't share our core values. So when you are ready for change, a great place to start is to create new core values and align them with your new mindset.

As the CEO of The Startup Business Factory, I'm asked many times when working with my clients, entrepreneurs, and business owners, what was the turning point for me? How did I go from living in the basement of my church member's house to living my dreams? And I'll tell you the same thing I told them:

I birthed a new mindset that changed everything for me. I realized that something had to change, and I was determined to make that change. I changed my environment to be around more positive people. I started going to church and that helped shift my mindset even further. Now that I have a new way of thinking, I can put my needs first, without being selfish. To fill others up, I must first be full. I can say no without feeling guilty. I can decline a request to be a part of certain organizations, programs, and events without feeling bad.

My new mindset has taught me not to be apologetic about considering my own needs. Now my entire life has shifted. I finally get it. I finally understand that my mentality gives birth to everything in my life and I attract what I think. I now have a very supportive husband and spiritual leader who is also my best friend and business partner, lovely children, a church family that we lead, and thriving businesses. This happened for me only by the grace of God and the mindset shift He birthed in me. Daily, I have to make the decision to walk in my newness. I'm being made new every day. I make a conscious choice to be better. My mindset changed. I changed. My mindset made me over. My mindset gave me life. My mindset gave me my joy back. My mindset gave me a future and a hope. My mindset gave me success. My mindset made me better. Now it's your time to move from broke to better.

See you at the top.

Trusting in Your Alpha and Omega

Chezline Riley

A devoted Christian, I am passionate about the ministries in which I serve, especially as they position me to help young people know God and aspire to their full potential. At my local church, I serve as the head of Youth Ministries, youth club counselor, and music coordinator/choir director, as well as choir member and soloist. I also tutor students in preparation for college level examinations. I know that God, my Alpha and Omega, who knows the end from any beginning, has placed me in these roles because He has a plan to use me in a marvelous way for His glory.

Having grown up in church, I've always *known about* God. And I always knew that the God of the Bible was bigger than anything this earth could ever produce. Yet, I've only recently discovered that I didn't fully *know* God, didn't truly understand the nature nor depth of His love for me, for *every* one of us. Have you ever felt like you've just been plodding through life playing the part of a good Christian only to realize that you're just a "churchgoer" enjoying that feel-good worship, yet you're not really comprehending the character nor fully committing to the

God you claim to serve? Or maybe you are in a place of unawareness, having heard about Him but having always wondered what all the fuss was about.

For me, it was the former. Despite the declaration in Hebrews 11:6 NIV that "without faith it is impossible to please God, because anyone who comes to him must believe that he exists and that he rewards those who earnestly seek him," I'd been walking through life thinking that I was a lone operative in solving my problems. We can be so blind at times, can't we? Everywhere we look, God presents clear evidence, from scripture as well as from life, of His love and willingness to provide for our needs, but somehow, we see through a glass darkly. God has had to forcibly move me out of my comfort zone and allow me to be broken so that He could reveal that He *wants* to bless me. He has shown up and delivered me through so many situations that I am now convinced that He is my Jehovah Jireh, the Omnipotent, Omniscient, and Omnipresent God.

Do you realize what it means to know that God is omniscient? It means that He who has numbered the very hairs on your head (Matthew 10:30) and who perceives your thoughts from afar and knows the word on your tongue before you even speak it (Psalms 139:1-4) has got your back. Literally, you can turn your back and say, "Lord, please take care of this or that and it's done." I'm saying God will turn your uncertain future into a certainty even when you can't fathom it.

I'd like to share this grand romanticized story of how I made a bold move to the United Kingdom to pursue my dreams and how God moved mightily in granting me the desires of my heart. But my story is not quite so exciting. I can, however, speak firsthand about God's provision in my life when I doubted, but even much more when I put my trust in His promises.

It's quite daunting, isn't it, when you endeavor to make a major move only to have people from all corners telling you what a big mistake you're making? And sometimes you're even tempted to fold and turn back from your decision. I've been there. My decision to immigrate to the United Kingdom was met with a great deal of negativity. Don't get me wrong—I had a few people who championed my cause and saw the move as a great way to explore a new horizon with new possibilities. But then there were the naysayers who kept insisting, even to the end, that England was a rough place to live.

Well, I'd be lying if I told you I didn't have my doubts. I experienced quite a bit of anxiety over this issue. I wondered if I'd be better off just settling with what I had in Montserrat even though I knew there was more I wanted and needed to explore. I wondered if I would reach the shores of Great Britain only to experience regrets and end up turning around and heading home. But then I decided to put my case before God. I told Him I didn't have a clue what I was about to encounter but left it in His capable hands.

In October 2013, just two weeks before I was due to leave for England, we got the call that my older sister, who had been living in England with my younger disabled brother, was in the hospital. She had been suffering for years from an overactive thyroid but was not consistently taking the medication. This all came to a head in a dramatic way one day, manifesting itself in some episodes of psychosis. She would have to remain in the hospital until the end of the month, so I rested in the knowledge that she would still be there when my brother, who had been vacationing in the United States at the time, and I arrived. However, when we got to her home in London, we were surprised and confused to see she'd already been discharged from the hospital. During the next few weeks, it was clear that she was still unwell. The family experienced many dark moments during that period. I cried out to God so many times and wondered if He heard me. As for my sister, she eventually felt compelled to leave the United Kingdom and return to our homeland, Montserrat, as she tried to get through the crisis.

Now, my disabled brother, having lost the only family member he'd come to depend on, was left bereft and scared and couldn't understand what had transpired or what was to happen to him. But this is where God shows His omniscience; He knew exactly what the outcome of my sister's plight would be. He knew that my brother's disabilities (speech and hearing impairments, blindness in one eye, and learning disability) meant that England was the place he, as a British citizen, needed to be, where he had access to the necessary medical care.

So the Alpha and Omega, the One who knows the beginning from the end, put me in place at just the right time so I could be there for my brother. Today, as I see how dependent he is on me for support of his needs—advocacy, advice, companionship, assistance with personal things, etc.—I'm glad I chose to trust God. If you never believed it before, believe it now: God sees and knows all things and is always working things out for our good, though in His time and His way, not ours.

What is it about us humans that makes us so fearful for the future when a little trouble comes, even when we say we believe in God? We experience these cycles of doubt and belief, discouragement and hopefulness, when we really have so much precedence in our own lives and in the lives of others to assure us that God is a God who says what He means and means what He says. Have you ever felt so overwhelmed with the cares of life that you seriously doubt whether God will actually deliver on His promise to never leave you nor forsake you? I certainly have many times in my life. Yet Matthew 6:26 ESV tells us that "the birds of the air: they neither sow nor reap...and yet your heavenly Father feeds them." If He provides even for the birds who are of lower value than man, how much more will He provide for His children whom He loves with an everlasting love?

Who do you run to in *your* time of need? What is your reaction when you don't see the answers to your questions or provisions for your needs manifesting themselves in the time frame you're expecting? Do you take desperate measures or "curse" God for not listening? I implore you to sit awhile at Jesus' feet and watch how He operates. The Great I Am who died on the cross to save us from eternal damnation will not see you suffer forever. He is ever making intercession on our behalf before the Father. Now you may have to endure for a season before your blessing comes but know that it's coming. My God, *our* God, is a God of love and He is ever seeking to bestow good things on us. All He asks is that we trust Him.

After arriving in England, I waited almost a year before I got a job, partially because the beginning was such a stressful time for me and my family. The other factor was that I was focusing so much on pursuing a teaching career since, after moving back to Montserrat, I'd really enjoyed the short stint teaching business during the three years I had spent there. Now, to become a qualified teacher, I would have had to enter a training program for a year in the classroom with little or no income and still be able to support myself. As a single woman living alone in a new town, that would prove rather challenging, so I eventually gave up that idea and began seeking other roles that were in line with my actual qualifications and experience. I applied mainly to institutions of higher education, as I wanted to remain in the education sector if not teaching, but the results were not very positive for a while.

In August 2014, I eventually found a job, which was a temporary, three-month role. After that, I took another temporary position for a year. Then in April 2016, I finally found a job that, not only do I enjoy, but which comes with so much promise, even though it doesn't lead to the career path I had in mind. Now, after being in a progressive career in higher education for over eleven years while living in the United States, this was a hard pill to have to swallow. Yet, for this breakthrough I count my blessings as God heard my cry and met my needs in a remarkable way.

But as you can imagine, the road to that outcome was anything but smooth. Quite the contrary. Yet it taught me so much about the way God works. All along the way, I met obstacle after obstacle, yet God kept providing the help I needed. Ensuring that my brother, who had secured a flat of his own in assisted independent living, was taken care of, I moved in with a family friend who sacrificed her bedroom so that I could be comfortable, a deed for which I was truly grateful. I stayed with her for seven months before moving into my own flat. I'll tell you, it wasn't easy. I would sometimes go weeks without doing any job hunting just because I was feeling so low and couldn't muster up the motivation to do a search. And so many nights I would just lie in bed and cry for my sister and the hardships she was enduring back at home. She would later learn the hard way what a grave mistake that move was. Also, to compound the situation, funds were running low by then. These were the times when I most needed the Lord but the times when I least prayed for myself. Oh, but God is good and He is faithful, even when we aren't! Let me tell you about my angel, whom the Lord has given to me.

Do you know what it is to have a genuine, consistent friend in your life? I mean a friend with no strings, no expectations? Well, some years ago, while I was living in the United States, God brought someone into my life whom I call my angel. She has been there for me at some very significant mileposts over the years. Once in England, whenever I was at my lowest ebb financially, just before I ran out of funds or really needed money to cover an important expense, this friend would either call or send me an email out of the blue saying, "Honey, I just put a little something into your account." Just like that. No asking whether I needed money or how much. She would just sense that I was in need. My friend is not religious in any way, but she is the epitome of that sentiment, "a friend in need is a friend indeed."

My God is an awesome God, yes He is! All this time, He was trying to teach me to rely on Him to be my Burden Bearer, my Jehovah Jireh, Provider of every need. You may not always get the things you want, but God knows what you need before you do and sets the wheels in motion to accomplish it before you can even conceive of a plan. From this experience, I began to see an increase in my faith. It is not just some talisman to be dangled in front of others to show I belong to God. It has become a living faith that I can see growing and transforming my character. It is what keeps the smile on my face and the spring in my step. It's what sends me to my knees when I sense trouble rather than going the route of fear. Do you want to experience that kind of joy in your life? Just put your hands in the hands of the Master and let him order your steps.

Amazingly but not surprisingly, last year, God revealed this rather powerful and even more compelling evidence of His power to move mountains. When my granddad died, I was faced with having to undertake all the funeral expenses on my own, a feat which was impossible with my human limitations. Yet, seeing no tangible sign of a breakthrough, I stood fast and pushed ahead with funeral plans. True to character, God showed up again mightily in the persons of not one but two angels, who selflessly moved in and virtually eliminated the burden of any funeral expense on my part.

I know when we are experiencing challenges that seem insurmountable, it's easy to forget who is Lord and Master of everything. But God has promised in His word that He will never leave the righteous forsaken nor His seed out begging for bread. My life is a living testament that He does work all things out for the good of those who love Him and are called according to His purpose. God can be trusted! Today I am in a job I love, I just moved into a new flat, and my sister is back in the United Kingdom where she can get the treatment she needs.

If you had the opportunity to rewrite your life story, what would the script look like? Very different, I would imagine. I would choose to walk a path where God has complete control. I let the cares and concerns of this world dictate my life and order my steps, and I allowed the enemy to have his way for far too long. But we can be grateful that God is a God of second chances, who knows every repentant heart, hears every petition. My sole desire is to serve my Master and to give him my complete trust even in times of uncertainty.

Our heavenly Father is waiting on you and me to come to Him and claim the multitude of blessings He has in store for us. Jeremiah 29:11 says, "'For I know the plans I have for you,' declares the LORD, 'plans to prosper you and not to harm you, plans to give you hope and a future.'" I cling to that very hope and it gives me a peace that passes all understanding. Let this be your desire, to let God lead in your life, to be the captain of your ship so that as you ride through the stormy waves, you can be assured that he's got your back.

Answered Prayers

Ranelli Williams

On Sunday, May 14, 2006, I called my mother to wish her Happy Mother's Day. We conversed with each other as we normally do. However, before the conversation was over, I found myself weeping and asking my mom, "When I am going to be a mother? Will that ever happen for me?"

Being the loving mother that she is, she begged me not to stress about it but to put my trust in God. She followed with a prayer like only a mother can pray, pleading with God to have mercy on her child, me, and to bless me with the desires of my heart to be a mother.

You see, I had been married for four years and, being in my mid-thirties, I thought time was running out. Little did I know that God's timing is not our timing. What we need to remember when we find ourselves in these types of situations is God's promise in Jeremiah 29:11, "'For I know the plans I have for you,' declares the Lord, 'plans to prosper you and not to harm you, plans to give you hope and a future.'" Also, Jeremiah 17:7-8 ESV says, "Blessed is the man who trusts in the Lord, whose trust is the Lord. He is like a tree planted by water, that sends out its roots by the stream, and does not fear when heat comes, for its leaves remain green, and is not anxious in the year of drought, for it does not cease to bear fruit."

After my mother's prayer, I felt a calm, a peace that passes all understanding. Through her prayer, God assured me that I would be a mother someday soon. My husband and I began to pray more diligently, but not only did we pray—we took action. We sought our doctor's expertise to figure out the reason for our infertility. Once we got our answer that part of the issue was that I had a blocked tube, we were already in such belief that God's promise would be manifested in our lives that our renewed faith did not waiver.

Our next step was to figure out what could be done. This was a big, bold move for us to even think about. You see, we are from a culture that often looks down on people who are childless, as if they have done something wrong. This is similar to how Job's friends asked him what he did to cause all the trouble he was going through. Not to mention the other set of "church folk" who would think that it's God's will, so let it be. However, we knew the conversations we'd had with God. We knew the conviction He placed in our heart, so we were ready for the journey. God led me to entrust what we were going through with one of my friends, who at the time wasn't even that intimate of a friend, but God chose her. Something in me said I could trust her.

Al-Nadeen prayed with me and she began a search for what could be the solution. Together, we identified a number of options, and after my husband and I took these options to God, only then did we move to find a specialist to work with. I know some of you might be wondering, where was our doctor in all of this? The answer is, he did his job. He told us what the issue was and mentioned we may need fertility treatments. His job was done. The rest was up to God, and God led us in the direction of our own research with the help of our friend.

Once we identified a fertility specialist, we made the visit, learned our best options, what our chances were of conceiving, and chose a course of action. Our next obstacle was figuring out how we would be able to afford the whopping $12,000 it would cost.

We immediately checked our medical policy and, to our amazement, the fertility treatments were covered. The exact course of action we decided to take was included in that coverage. Can we say "confirmation"? We did not have to pay anything out of pocket except for copays. Praise the Lord!

The course we chose was IVF, and if you check the statistics, many people try multiple times before being successful or not being successful at all. For us, our first try was a success. Imagine the joy both my husband and I experienced when we got the call that I was pregnant. We celebrated and praised God like we had never before.

Imagine if we had cowered in fear about what people would think. And to some extent, we did because we chose not to share or even solicit the prayers of our church family as we were going through this process. But we trusted God. We were confident that He had led us down this path, and we boldly followed His direction. In August 2007, our first son Joeraan was born and we could not have been happier. Our belief resulted in our big blessing. However, as Joeraan began to speak and see others with siblings, he started asking for a brother or sister. My husband and I both came from a large family, so we did not want him to be an only child. At first, I was afraid to encourage Joeraan's prayers because I knew I would not go through another IVF procedure. Financially, it cost too much, and the year after Joeraan was born, fertility was no longer covered under our medical plan. Coincidence? I think not. So that option was off the table for us, and because we didn't think we would be able to conceive naturally, in our minds, that was off the table as well.

But in speaking with God about how to handle my son asking and praying for a sibling, the answer came clearly to me: encourage his prayers. And so I did. I didn't want to disappoint him, but I heard clearly, *encourage his prayers!* Every night, Joeraan would pray for a brother, and then he would switch his prayer and ask for a sister. He didn't care what it was; he just wanted a sibling. Eric and I prayed as well and started considering adoption. We even started the preliminary processes. We thought this would be God's answer to our prayers.

In March 2012, I went with my church family to a women's retreat. At that retreat, we were encouraged to write on a board our one big prayer request that we were seeking God for. Well, you know what mine was: a sibling for Joeraan. We prayed over these requests in sincerity and I believed my prayer was answered. I went back home after that weekend and, six weeks later, when I had no menstruation, I was puzzled. Since we had already started to move in the direction of adoption, I thought that was the answer and that I couldn't possibly be pregnant. I immediately wondered if I was sick and also pondered, could I be? I made an appointment with my OBGYN, which was three weeks out.

After a week, I could not wait any longer. I ran to the drugstore and bought a pregnancy test. It was positive. I screamed for my husband to come to the bathroom. Once I showed it to him, he was in shock. We were both in shock. There was a second test strip with the package so the next morning I repeated the test. It was positive again. Could this be? When? How? Was it even possible? Two weeks later, my visit to my OBGYN confirmed that I was indeed pregnant. God worked a miracle and in December 2012, our second son, Jaevaan, was born. What a mighty God we serve. He may not come when we want Him, but He is always on time.

I pray this testimony blesses you. I pray that you know that when things seem impossible, God has a plan, and He is working everything out for your good. Be encouraged. He is a God of possibilities. Put the case in God's hands, ask, seek, and knock, and watch Him work a miracle in your life.

BOLD REDISCOVERY

Six Faith Walkers Share Their Journey to Peace and Fulfillment After Broken Relationships

My Favorite Was My Fear

Marcella D. Moore

As a little girl, I knew that there was something unique about me. I wanted to teach anyone who would listen. I would go down in the basement of my parent's home, lie on the floor, and start making learning sheets with math, spelling, and writing. I would gather the girls in my neighborhood and family and braid their hair because I wanted them to feel good about themselves. I knew that there was something different about me, but I could not identify it nor did I want to. I always knew that I wanted to help people and make them feel good about themselves, but there was nothing in me that wanted to do it in front of people. I was going to save the world from the comfort of my home and in my backyard.

The first time I heard Marianne Williamson's words from her book, I fell in love with each word. Below is my favorite quote:

"Your playing small does not serve the world. There is nothing enlightened about shrinking so that other people won't feel insecure around you. We are all meant to shine, as children do."

These words became my mantra as I was rediscovering myself after accepting the fact that after seventeen years of marriage, I was now a single mother responsible for raising my ten-year-old daughter and six-year-old son. At that stage in my life, all I knew was how to be my ex-husband's wife and children's mother. After years of feeling abandoned, alone, and pitiful, I made a decision to become a part of my own rescuing and live again. The words from Ms. Williamson served as my guide. As a woman of faith, I believed that God was with me and He had a divine purpose for my life. As I continued on my journey to self-discovery, I became more confident and began to love myself again. My level of self-confidence and esteem was limited, but it would be at an all-time high as long as I was helping others backstage or behind the scenes.

I was always the person in my family and with my friends who prayed for and encouraged others. One day in 2013, I texted eight of my family members and friends, who I connected with often, and asked, if I started a conference call on Saturday mornings at eight to pray with them and encourage them, would they call? They all said yes. My goal was to create one time and place where I could talk to all of them at once. It was fun, effective, and intimate.

After a couple of weeks, someone asked if they could invite a friend. Then every week I'd get a text message from someone saying that their friend would be joining the call on Saturday. My answer was always yes until one day I realized that it was no longer just myself and eight others. At that time of conference calling, you had to set up the line in advance and assign a certain number of participants. I started getting nervous; it was one thing to talk to family and friends—those who I was familiar with—but now people who didn't know me would be hearing my voice.

Within a couple of weeks, I was locking in up to twenty-five participants so I said, that's it. I made an announcement on the call that we were at our maximum, never identifying what that number was to the callers.

I found myself going back to Ms. Williamson's words, quoting over and over, "Your playing small does not serve the world." I heard the words loud and clear, and although I believed in my favorite words, I was not going to increase the number of people who could join the call. Besides, I was caring for my mother who was diagnosed with lung cancer and this reasoning justified my thought process to keep my circle small.

That summer, I met my sister and friend, who is still a very important part of my life today. Here lies my faith walker's journey. She spoke at an event I attended and afterwards we shared our lives with each other and discovered that we had many things in common regarding life and ministry. As we were wrapping up our conversation, I mentioned the Saturday morning call and how it had started with nine of us but every week, people wanted to invite others, and I was not opening the lines. She looked at me (without knowing my favorite words) and said, "God said stop playing small and that you better take the limits off of Him."

Those words stuck with me. I went home that evening and sat on the floor in my bedroom with tears running down my face, asking God to forgive me for quoting Ms. Williamson's words all this time and not willing to live them. In that moment, I realized that I called these words my favorite, but they were really my fear. Fear, as it pertains to my story, is the belief in your mind that you can't, you shouldn't, and you are not capable of doing something because you are not skilled enough, strong enough, and powerful enough to do so. It's the thought that stops you from moving because you don't know what's going to happen.

As often as I quoted the words to others and felt empowered every time I said them, fear had overtaken me and would not allow me to grow. The fear was the blocker of my expansion. I often prayed the prayer of Jabez:

> And Jabez called on the God of Israel, saying, Oh that thou wouldest bless me indeed, and enlarge my coast, and that thine hand might be with me, and that thou wouldest keep *me* from evil, that it may not grieve me! And God granted him that which he requested (1 Chronicles 4:10 KJV).

Asking God to expand my territory, I often read out loud Deuteronomy 28: "If you fully obey all of these commandments of the Lord your God, the laws I am declaring to you today, God will transform you into the greatest nation in the world." I gave fear a full ride on my purpose, dreams, and visions. While talking to God that day, I asked Him what He wanted from me concerning this call: what was this call really about and what was He doing?

He simply said to me, "I want you to *motivate* and I want you to *pray*," and that was the true birthing of Motivate and Pray. Although He told me what to do, I still wasn't sure of what Motivate and Pray would become, but I knew that in order to find out, I had to push through my fear and begin to walk by faith. Each day, I realized that God gave me this ministry and movement as a support mechanism and igniter. That night, I quoted the words from "Our Deepest Fear," and they took on a new meaning for me.

The next day, I did my research and found a new conference call line that allowed up to 1,000 participants. Today, we have callers from all around the country. As mentioned earlier, during this Motivate and Pray birthing process, I was caring for my mother. On my caregiver journey, I sought for a support group that would help encourage me when I was feeling overwhelmed, and I could not find one. Opening myself for expansion and pushing through fear gave me the courage to start the Caring for the Caregiver Network, a support network for caregivers who are caring for sick and aging family members or friends and special needs children.

The moment I surrendered to divine purpose and truly saw myself the way God sees me, my favorite words took on a new meaning. Illumination, revelation, and a true understanding of who I really am manifested in me. The moment God gives you a dream, vision, calling, or goal, He qualifies you for it. Our job is to fine tune and develop that dream, vision, calling, or goal by educating ourselves, surrendering to God's will, and trusting Him to lead and direct us as we walk through the process.

Can I encourage you just for a moment to not think about what you don't have or what you can't do but instead think about the ability you have to be great? Your greatness comes with an ability to shine, grow, increase, and walk out your purpose with courage and confidence. I, just like you, had the inkling that something big was inside of me, but because I looked at my circumstances and imposed my limitations and imbalanced beliefs, I could not see the light and jewel that I was. The moment I allowed God to open my eyes, my new vision allowed me to not only see my light but to become the light and allow that light to shine in a way that would cause babies to leap, sleeping giants to awake, and hearts to open.

What I learned in this process is that God is a big God and everything that He has invested in us is as big as He is. I, because I did not remember who I was, created this limited life that kept me in a comfort zone and blocked me from being the true light God had called me to be. Had I remained comfortable in this not-so-purposeful space, it would have stopped me from touching the lives of those who were assigned to me the moment I entered this earth. I limited myself, I played small because it felt safe and secure, and my shrinking hindered the blessings that were trying to find their way to me. God did not create Motivate and Pray to consist of myself and nine others; He created it to touch the lives of those throughout the country. Because I said yes, caregivers from all over the country are empowered on a monthly basis; because I said yes, the Dreamgirls Workshop was born and it encourages women to become dream makers. Because I refused to believe the lie that said I was better off staying small because it's safer and that no one really wanted to hear me, testimonies of healing, love, employment, restoration, and reconciliation are received weekly.

If you are a business owner and are limiting yourself, if you are a single parent and feel like you cannot follow your dreams because of your status, if you are caring for a sick family member or friend and feel like there is no hope, if you are celebrating your forties, fifties, or sixties and feel like you are too old to be great, if you know that there is something in you that's crying out for more, or if you just choose to believe the lie that says you can't do it, I want to speak life to you today. I want to encourage you to stop allowing fear to paralyze you from walking in your purpose. You will discover as I did that fear is present most of the time, but you have to do it, even with the fear. I want to remind you that you were designed for greatness. You have the ability to be great and shine in every arena that you are in. If God placed you there, He is prepared to give you the tools that you need to be successful there. You were not made to be small or live a little life; what you were created for is something big, and it is searching for you; it is screaming your name, and it wants to become your favorite, not your fear. Choose life and choose abundance. Start your faith walk journey today.

Dress for Change: Reposition Yourself to Soar

Stephnie A. Gregory

I am a single, energetic mother, motivator, and entrepreneur with a passion to mentor and educate people so that they can develop life skills to be successful and to reach their goals. My motto in life is to stay focused and to keep my eyes on the prize. I believe that each person has the ability to accomplish whatever they desire once she or he finds their niche and develops the required skills.

As I journey through this life, I strive to emulate positivity so that I can be a role model to my community and my peers. I have learned that listening to others makes the best learning experiences. Being focused, having a plan, and keeping your eyes on the prize is my motto for success. In life, you have to believe in yourself and believe that each person possesses a special gift. As Albert Einstein stated, "Everyone is a genius. But if you judge a fish by its ability to climb a tree, it will live its whole life believing that it is stupid."

In this life, there is no such thing as luck. Hard work makes you successful. I learned early that preparation meets opportunity, which leads to achieving goals toward the next level. It is because of my belief and trust in God that I possess the strength and determination to prepare me for what life has to offer.

My faith was tested after ten years of marriage. I woke up one day and my life had changed from the stroke of a pen. I became a statistic in the court of law and traveled on the road called Divorce. I realized that I was not alone, that others were walking this long and winding road with many roadblocks and potholes of all sizes. I was comforted by Psalms 55:22: "Cast thy burden upon the Lord, and he shall sustain thee: he shall never suffer the righteous to be moved."

As I continued to hold onto God's grace, I realized that you have to put your trust in God first and not man. Daily, God reminds me over and over never to fear, as you are prepared and already dressed for the change. What does that mean? It does not mean wearing a suit or beautiful makeup. It means that I have already developed my self-independence and self-esteem, and that I am motivated, focused, and prepared to handle any struggles that come my way. I realized that after my divorce, the time had come for me to fully utilize all the principles that I developed throughout my life to move me to the next level. To God be the glory, great things He has done.

Every day, I am determined to view life's challenges as opportunities. Personally, setting goals daily helped me to strategically map out my life and work within a specific time frame to achieve my accomplishments. I firmly believe that in order to be successful, one must plan and outline his or her path and put God first; all other things will come to light. There were times when I would lose faith and think that the whole world was against me, but God sees our future and He knows what time to take control. I learned when I pray to let go and trust Him, believe, and wait. He knows when, where, how, and exactly what we need to do to move forward in life. Through the change in my life, there was not one day I questioned God by asking "why me?" The journey was not mine. I knew He was preparing me for bigger and greater things, and I had to believe and take bold steps to overcome the obstacles that confronted me and to continue to plant more seeds in preparation for change.

As a single parent, raising a seven-year-old daughter was not an easy task. I taught her to be independent and to be a leader, not a follower. I have helped her develop values such as self-respect, which reminds her to always respect others and to treat them as she would want to be treated. With the principles she developed, she became a guidance counselor and deputy head girl for her school and was admired by her peers.

Preparing for my future meant equipping myself academically. After leaving high school, I went straight into the work field and became comfortable and content with no desire to pursue higher education. I kept thinking my job was secure as I was advancing in my career. Soon after, during a conversation with a fellow employee, he said to me, "You will never receive a management position in this organization."

I was stunned by this statement. I looked at him and said, "Why would you say that?"

He responded, "You don't have a degree!"

His response, however disturbing, was realistic. Those words kept resounding in my mind, and I realized that I had to make a change. God places people in our lives for a reason, and that reason is to deliver the message. When we pray, we have to ask God to give us the wisdom to identify His messengers to allow us to listen, as He sends the word in different forms.

Within two weeks, I registered for and pursued several management courses with a college. I successfully completed the program, and I was given a senior role on the job. We have to constantly dress ourselves for change in order to reposition our lives. These words from Henry Wadsworth Longfellow serve as a source of inspiration to me: "The heights by great men reached and kept were not attained by sudden flight, but they, while their companions slept, were toiling upward in the night." I continued on to a degree program and spent sleepless nights completing assignments and pledged to remain focused in order to earn the required credits to obtain the degree. It was very difficult having a full-time job, being a single parent, and pursuing a four-year degree. This meant exercising time management, but I was determined.

Realizing that I needed to move on in life, I started going back full-time to church and gradually got myself involved in groups where I could help to make a difference. I was given an opportunity to speak at a women's conference. I recalled that I declined the invitation because I felt depressed and feared what others would say. It took me three weeks before I could respond to the invitation. I prayed, asking God, is it Your will? Eventually, I heard the spirit of the Lord speaking to me to empower the women to believe in themselves, be bold, and allow God to bless them unconditionally and to continue to walk in faith.

I was truly blessed as God gave me the strength to deliver His word. I watched the women as they listened intently as I explained that, as believers in God, we have to change our mindset and reposition ourselves to make a difference in our lives. I encouraged them to never cease praying and at the same time take action and continue to be the gatekeepers of their lives and be ready for change. My message served as a source of inspiration as I told my story, encouraging them to pay attention to their behavioral patterns so that they could identify changes and, most importantly, listen for the unspoken words.

In life, we are surrounded by the blame game or the many excuses why we do not take responsibility for our actions; rather, we find every excuse instead of looking in the mirror. I wonder what is holding us back from making independent decisions for empowerment. Is it fear of the unknown or lack of confidence? Confidence is developed when we prepare ourselves to face the unknown. Preparation begins with the mindset, as we focus on how we can position ourselves to take full control of our lives. We all have control of our destiny by the choices we make.

I committed to becoming a leader for Girl Guides, which is an organization that enables girls to develop themselves and trains them to become responsible citizens. Girls between the ages of ten to fifteen years join this organization, seeking guidance in self-development and career preparation. This organization challenges them professionally and personally as they focus on leadership skills, teamwork, goal setting, people skills, working with the community, and enjoying outdoor activities. I have had the privilege of working with these girls and watch them grow and develop into responsible citizens. I eventually retired from Girl Guides leadership and relocated to begin the next chapter in my life.

I continued my journey in life, and I pursued my dream of becoming an entrepreneur. Ever since I knew myself, I always had a desire to become a business owner. I had no idea how to begin the steps of owning my own business but continued to remain optimistic that one day it would happen. My opportunity came when I least expected it, when someone asked me to join a direct-selling business. The investment was a one-time startup fee of $10.00, and without even thinking, I accepted the invitation and said yes. As Richard Branson, owner of Virgin Atlantic said, "If someone offers you an amazing opportunity but you are not sure you can do it, say yes—then learn how to do it later!" And that is exactly what I did. I learned fast. Today, I am eternally grateful for that opportunity to be part of a billion-dollar company. I am growing and mentoring a team to empower others, and working with the team allows me to learn about the diversity of culture and strengthen relationships with each team member.

I developed a simple formula to get through the trials and tribulations of life. It helps me reflect and serves as a guide in an effort to remain focused, committed, dedicated, and passionate. It takes a lot of sacrifice. I know that I have learned to put God first and to pray without ceasing. Prayer changes things. I let God take over because the battle is not mine. I encourage everyone to always be prepared for life's changes, be empowered, and never, never give up on themselves. I once read this quote: "In life, many things don't go according to plan. If you fall, get back up. If you stumble, regain your balance. Never give up."

Today, I am happy I traveled the path that was prepared for me. It took me to a place where I realized my potential, and I am presently using my talent to continue to help others who are making decisions that will allow them to progress in life. I have met some wonderful people along the way who have played an integral part in my life. Most importantly, I know that I could not survive alone if it had not been for my parents and family who supported me throughout the change process. They have been my anchor and would always give me the positive side of every direction to take. Their words of wisdom will always remain with me as I continue to progress on life's journey.

All Things Are Beautiful in Time

Angela Pizarro

As a young girl, I was fascinated with fairy tales, particularly Cinderella. It wasn't just a love story to me but a rags-to-riches story, where the underdog triumphs. Cinderella was the "least of these," as quoted in the Bible. But fate seemed kind in the end. True love pursued her, and soon, she and the handsome prince lived happily ever after.

I too had similar dreams of being a success against all odds. I dreamed about having plenty of children and adoration. As life went on, I wasn't very confident in my appearance or intelligence. I was born and raised in Brooklyn, New York. I was skinny, and my face resembled pizza, so kids in school called me "pizza face," which was a play on my last name, Pizarro. Children can be so cruel at times.

High school wasn't any better as competition was prevalent in the all-girl school I attended. I decided that the right guy could make all the difference in the world for me and make me feel special. Having little to no confidence, and on the rebound from my high school heartbreak, I married my best friend.

My fairy tale relationship didn't quite work out as I had envisioned, and I found myself pregnant and afraid. We were young and foolish, and the sudden marriage ended before it ever started. Alcohol and infidelity, as well as financial ruin, led me to divorce court shortly after. Life had gotten so complicated, but somehow, I knew that things had to get better.

I was raised in a Christian environment, and although my parents would have welcomed me home, I was determined to make it on my own. Public assistance became the saving grace for my daughter and me.

I didn't have time to think or reflect on my choices because there was no time for depression or regret. I guess I was afraid of seeing how much time had passed by and the reality of how much time was wasted. So I did not make it my focus.

I always thought that tomorrow would be a better day, an opportunity to get it right. I didn't realize it at the time, but God knew the plans He had for me. He had plans for a future and not plans for my demise. It wasn't long before I married again and had three beautiful boys. Life was good. We moved into our first home, and we even had a dog! My fairy tale life had materialized finally, or so I thought.

Wherever we lived had always been a place where others felt comfortable. There could be at any time a dozen children in my house, which I welcomed. Some would stay for months while their mothers repaired their lives, while others who came from very dysfunctional situations would come by daily. I fed them, ministered to them, cried with them, and loved them.

As bills added up, I began to work two jobs to try and help make ends meet. My husband and I chose to work hours that allowed one of us to always be home for our children. I soon found myself sleep deprived, as four hours was all the time I could steal many days.

I was active in my church: I led worship and joined many different study groups. I volunteered for overtime at work and stretched myself so thin, it's a wonder I didn't have a heart attack. I should have been happy with my life, but something was desperately wrong. I felt out of control.

My marriage basically resembled two ships passing in the night, and I felt constant guilt that I wasn't doing enough or giving my marriage enough attention. There was never enough money, and as arguing took the place of conversation, things seemed hopeless. I cried myself to sleep many days and nights, and there wasn't anyone who would understand or relate to my situation.

After ten years, we lost our home. We found an apartment, but we had to get rid of our family dog. Fighting depression, I found myself praying and fasting in need of some hope. My health had been suffering, and I received negative reports of chronic acid reflux, heart palpitations, and anemia. My diet consisted of fast food and too much coffee and sugar, which I had to consume regularly to stay awake. Several car accidents were soon to follow as a result of my strenuous lifestyle. Too tired to fall asleep and too worried to stay asleep was how I spent my days and nights.

Because I neglected it, my health continued to decline. I had to leave my two jobs and was put on several medications as well as undergo surgeries to repair the damage time had done to my body. Time grew to be an enemy to me because I couldn't see how it was ever in my favor. I desperately wished for more hours in a day! I had become a "time-aholic," complaining that there was never enough of it.

When I was forced to stop working, I resembled a junkie trying to kick a drug habit! I felt like I no longer had purpose. I needed a miracle as life felt like a merry-go-round that I needed to jump off. My miracle came in the way of my acceptance and awareness that I needed to change my mindset about everything, and as I began to accept my fate, things started to look up.

Being at home afforded me the opportunity to work on my jewelry, something I had never had time for. Another benefit was walking. I couldn't do anything too strenuous, and I was diagnosed as morbidly obese. Walking became therapy. As I walked, I came across so many people who needed prayer as well as offering prayer. The homeless and others who needed love filled my days with prayer and love once again. I began to lose weight, I gained confidence in myself, and my faith in God was strengthened as I started to see myself the way God sees me: valuable, smart, and worth dying for!

Once life seemed to be turning around for the better, I received the call from my sister that my father's health took a turn for the worse; he was suffering from dementia and other health issues. As we sat around his bedside, my mind rushed back to my childhood when I would sit in his workshop as he tinkered with something. He loved for me to share my dreams with him. He was such a good listener and would happily encourage me to be anything I wanted. We would create things together and my imagination would soar as we both loved to craft and create.

I struggled to let go and accept that my father was going to a much better place. My life had changed drastically after he went home to be with the Lord. All that could have been shaken was shaken.

As I was dealing with the loss of my hero, I received news that a surrogate daughter I had known for thirteen years had tragically died in a car accident, leaving behind her twin sister. Two funerals in a week. I had to encourage her and her family while grieving with mine. I don't know how I held up. Only God held me together. His grace truly is sufficient, but I didn't see it at the time.

What was time doing? How could it be so cruel?

I lay out before the Lord, sobbing and asking Him how I could go on. I had no control of life, death, or time. The truth of the matter is, I had tried to cheat time. I stole bits and pieces, taking for granted that tomorrow would always come. That my loved ones would always be there and that I could always make up for lost time. But I soon learned that time won't stand still for anyone.

It didn't for two loved ones, and I refused to let any more time slip away on what didn't count. Something changed in me. I don't know at what point I finally started to take back my life and start to live from a place of victory, but I knew life couldn't and wouldn't be the same ever again.

The loss of my dad and my surrogate daughter were the catalyst God used to shake me free from sitting at the starting line to being an active participant in the race called life! I can truly say that God delivered me out of fear of failure to a place of hope and confidence. I was still alive and while I had breath, there was so much I needed to do! I can now say God truly works all things together for my good. My faith has not only been restored but it has increased! Faith trumps time every time!

It was truly God who helped me to salvage the relationships that were estranged with my children, and it is He who will take me through the other trials in my life. This newfound hope, despite life's tests, came as a result of the renewing of my mind. I had blamed time when all my experiences and choices were not a surprise to God. Every valley as well as every mountain was necessary to be traveled in order to learn and earn my testimony and tell my story. We are all connected and our stories should help one another. Nothing is wasted. No time is lost. I had to first surrender to His plan and trust in His power, not my own. I was ordained as a minister and now pastor those who God sends my way. And out of all this, my jewelry business, TreClara, was finally birthed.

Time is nothing to God—He controls it and owns it! I am enjoying my newfound freedom, and my life will never be the same. At the present time, I am amazed by all God is doing in my life! I have never stopped writing or dreaming. I am working on another book that will address and uncover lies we all believe and free your spirit to soar. And God hasn't stopped there! I am embarking on speaking engagements as well as continuing my education in counseling and ministry.

God does answer prayers! I live by the passage in the word of God, found in Ecclesiastes 3:11: "He hath made every thing beautiful in his time: also he hath set the world in their heart, so that no man can find out the work that God maketh from the beginning to the end."

I pray that my story is an encouragement to someone. Your story may be worse than mine, or it may not be as bad as mine—it really doesn't matter. You are not a mistake and it is never too late for you to live out your dreams. God loves you, and He is too good to ever let you go. He is working it all together for your good—your mistakes as well as your triumphs. Your life can be a masterpiece if you put your faith in the Master of time. When you feel like you have let time slip away, remember that God's concept of time is not like ours. He is patient. Trust Him and put your faith in Him. He will show you how your faith can trump time all the time. All things truly are beautiful in its time! Be blessed!

The Aftermath Healing

Khalima Green

At that point of my life, I was already dedicated to the Lord. I considered myself a babe in Christ, however, because of my experience with separating from my husband and God opening new doors for me, my worship level changed. Chains were broken, strongholds destroyed, breakthroughs released, and my relationship with the Lord became stronger.

My husband and I were expecting. I was pregnant again. It was supposed to be one of the happiest moments in my life, but I wasn't happy. I was brokenhearted from three miscarriages. I was finally carrying full-term, and my husband and I were separated while living in the same house. We went from lovers to strangers and only communicated about bills. It was sad, but it was a reality I wasn't ready for, nor one I wanted.

The separation happened so fast and felt so surreal. I never thought in a million years that I would be going through that. I tried to stay positive; I did not want to stress myself. I was diagnosed with a high-risk pregnancy, so I wanted to maintain a healthy pregnancy even though I spent most of my days crying in secret and experiencing many emotions. *Lord, why me? How I am going to do this?* I made okay money, but was it going to be enough to provide for my children? I had a plan, but God had a better plan.

A couple of months later, my husband moved out. I thought I was going to miss him terribly. And I did at first; however, it was not as bad as I thought it would be and in some sense, it felt like a burden was lifted. I did not realize until later that things were actually falling into place instead of falling apart. My mother-in-law decided to stay with me and help me out. What a blessing. I was already in a position working from home (something I had always wanted), and I had family and friends in my corner supporting and encouraging me. It's so interesting that a person can have all the love and support and still feel abandoned. I may have been experiencing many emotions, but bills had to be paid, school work had to be done (I was a college student), and my oldest son needed his mother. So I continued to push.

I understood that if you want answers and need God to make some things clear to you, you fast and pray. By that point, I had done multiple corporate fasts with my church but never on my own. I did not understand that the fasts were simply to help with obedience, and God himself had to show me that. So I learned to fast and to pray effectively and not only read the word but study the word. Not only did He show me how to incorporate that into my lifestyle, but He also showed me that my son came at a perfect time. I didn't understand why God would allow my child to come at the point when my marriage was going down the drain. I had to realize that God is not a genie. I know it sounds funny, but we all do it: pray to God for whatever we want, and when He gives it to us, because it doesn't come at the time we want it, we don't want it anymore.

My ex-husband and I were praying for this child to come because we had multiple miscarriages, and we couldn't grasp in our mind that this child would come in the midst of our separation. God has a sense of humor. I was able to put aside what I was going through and allow myself to fall in love all over again. I fell in love with my unborn child. It had been thirteen years since I had last bared a child. I was excited and nervous at the same time. I wanted to be a better mother. I wanted to do things with my second child that I had not gotten to experience with my first.

The first thing I did was find the perfect name. I wanted a strong biblical name. One night while at Bible study, it dawned on me as we were studying the book of Nehemiah. What better name to have than Nehemiah, which means "comfort by Yahweh"? That's exactly what I was experiencing. I was going through my storm, but the baby was being comforted.

As I continued to seek God and prepare myself for this child, I focused on personal development. I attended a women's conference, and the guest speaker shared her testimony about her experience with her marriage and what she went through and how she had to realize the role she needed to play as a godly wife. She went into detail about how she was carrying the burden on herself and trying to do everything, meaning her role and his role as well, and she burnt herself out trying to do so; and then it hit me. I started to reflect on some things that had taken place in my marriage. I thought about the part I played and how I handled certain situations, acting as a single parent and making decisions without including my husband because I was a single parent before my husband came into my life. For the first time in my life, I saw things completely differently. I broke down and repented to God. I thought about everything that I had done over the years and thought, maybe if I had done things differently, I would have seen different results. I know I cannot turn back the hands of time, but I know I can make better and wiser decisions moving forward.

Prior to this experience happening, I told the Lord that I surrendered to Him, and He is allowed to have His way and to use me. Many of us have stated that, but how many of us mean it? Well, from that point on to now, I mean it. I had to stop running from the Lord and start allowing him to do the complete makeover in me. Once I did that, it was like the weight was taken off of me. This continued throughout the course of my pregnancy. Friends and family members noticed the change. I actually started to feel better about myself, and my confidence was blooming. Like I said, I had these qualities before, but this was the next level, all because I trusted God and allowed Him to seek me through.

Around this time in my life, God showed me through a dream that He had a double blessing for me. I was so excited, and I was ready to receive it. I waited, months went by, and nothing. I thought, okay, Lord, where is my blessing? No response. I finally said to myself, I guess in due time He will reveal it. I still continued to feed myself with the word. As the birth of my son started to get closer, I sent up a prayer request. I asked God to allow me to spend time with my new baby. My goal was to be home with my son during his first year, as I did not get a chance to experience that with my oldest son. I was only able to stay home with him for four months before having to go back to working two jobs.

When my second son Nehemiah was born, I was working from home, however, the type of work I was doing required me to be on the phone constantly, and all I wanted was time with my little man. I had two months with him without work, but that was not enough for me. I was praying to God to allow me to spend more time with my son. I was praying for a vehicle to allow me to create my own schedule. I went back to work for three weeks, and shortly afterward, I hurt my back and was out of work for two months. Now, that is not how I imagined spending time with my son, but sometimes we have to understand that things happen. I took it as my blessing in disguise. As I stated above, I was working from home, and I was at the point where I was no longer satisfied with that position. I wanted more. I was looking for an opportunity to work for myself, and I constantly prayed to God for that to happen.

Ever since I was a little girl, I had known that I wanted my own business. I was not sure where exactly I wanted to be, but I just knew I enjoyed learning about finance, and I also wanted to teach other people about finance and business. I liked the idea of working as an independent consultant/contractor, and I held many positions over the years. It was great to have multiple experiences in different areas such as customer service, healthcare, home healthcare, and catering, yet those jobs were not fulfilling. I wanted something that was fulfilling. In the meantime, I continued to apply for different positions at my job, however, the positions were not offered to me. I would get upset and go right back to God and tell him how I couldn't stand my job and that I wanted to be released. God is good all the time.

Five months later, I was released from that job of four years along with unemployment compensation. I had the opportunity to be a mother while still going to school, which I found to be very rewarding. I was able to create my own schedule to allow me to make time for schoolwork and to be there for my family I was able to take my son to his extracurricular activities, travel to see family, and enjoy my summer. But even though I enjoyed being at home, I still was pondering my career. I continued to pray to God to open doors for me, to put the right people in my path, and for me to be receptive to new opportunities.

One day, a friend of mine invited me to a women's networking event via Facebook. I hesitated at first, but I accepted the request and attended. The meeting was based on financial education. I loved it. I met some amazing women, and it was just what I was looking for. God is so good. Thereafter, I went to a couple of meetings because I was interested to see how I could be a part of this organization and become an independent representative.

Around the same time, my pastor was looking for help with the church's retreat center. At first, the tasks were simple, like taking calls and helping here and there, and then one day it dropped in my spirit that I wanted more. I had a conversation with the pastor, gave her my inputs, and said that I wanted to do so much more for the retreat center. She was very excited and she gave me the opportunity to take my ideas and run with them. And that's how my adventure started in my new contractual position as a marketing director. I love it. I can work from home and still attend business events and meetings.

The first event I attended to promote the retreat center was the 2016 L.I.F.T. Conference. I learned valuable information and the opportunity to learn about this book project. That was another thing I prayed to God about—writing a book. Isn't He awesome?

Everything I have shared all happened within a two-year time frame, and all I did was focus on God and how to make my future better. It felt like it took forever to come but it came. I have been restored, and my mind has been renewed. This life-changing event molded and shaped me. My Father was preparing me, and there is more to come. I am not perfect, but I am obedient. I may have not been patient all the time, but I was faithful because I knew He would provide. Look how everything flowed for me. I recognize my double blessing: the career change and the things I wanted for my children. If He can do it for me, He can do it for you.

Sometimes we think, "God, why are these things happening to me?," "I thought you had my back," "Where are you"? But I come to tell you that sometimes you have to look at the little things. It may not happen exactly how you want it, but He gives it to you. In my case, even though my husband and I are no longer together, God gave me what no one can give me, which is two beautiful boys, peace, hope, joy, a roof over my head, and support by my loved ones. He helped me transition from working for somebody else to working for myself, the big blessing I had been praying for. What a mighty God we serve!

My Daughter, a Gift from God

Ohilda Holguin

I am a dreamer, a giver, and I empower women to find their true selves. I help women heal from trauma and limiting beliefs by connecting them to their God-given spirit and giving them tools to remove any blocks that keep them separated from their relationship with the Lord.

Similar to other women, I wanted a great marriage, children, and an amazing career. However, I never asked God what He wanted for my life. I did not consult Him in any decision that I made, and only called on Him when I didn't get what I wanted, was desperate, or in pain. Can you relate? I had a limiting belief that I was not worthy. This belief affected many of my relationships, including my marriage.

In 2005, my husband and I went to New York, where I am from, to visit my family for Christmas. We had been married for four years, and let's just say that his gifts to me were a little tacky or not my taste. I appreciated them but did not love them. However, on this day, as I stood in his arms on Riverside Drive, with a slight wind blowing through my hair, I was the happiest woman alive. He gave me the most expensive and beautiful gift he had ever given me: a pair of diamond earrings.

As he opened the box, he uttered, "You are my queen, I love you!"

I felt like the happiest woman on earth. When we live life believing that material possessions are important, we forget that what is most important is to have a happy and loving home.

The next morning, an argument arose. My husband was extremely upset and decided to leave. He told me he was going back home to Florida. I was so confused. We had tickets to leave the next day. He walked out. I thought to myself, he is upset, he will take a walk and come back. That was around ten in the morning. I didn't tell anyone anything, and when my family came over for our going away dinner, I told them he was with friends. He didn't have a cell phone, and I didn't know where he was. By 10 p.m., I started to get extremely worried. I called his sister in Florida, told her what had happened and asked her to please call me if she heard from him. Shoot, he may have gone back to Florida. I had no idea. During all this time, I did not pray once. I did not ask the Lord for guidance. Finally, my husband showed up at 3 a.m. and didn't say a word.

The next day, I didn't say much. He told me he had called his local union brothers (he was an ironworker) and spent the day with them. He proceeded to tell me that he did not want to talk to me during the trip back home. I was so confused. What had happened? Even then, I did not pray. I had lost my relationship with the Lord somewhere down the line. I had forgotten that I could go to Him. It is important to remember that God is always with you, and you can count on Him. Depend on Him. Cast your worries onto Him.

A week later, as we were preparing to move into our first house, he told me he wanted a divorce. That same week, I got laid off from my job. We had given up the apartment we lived in so I found myself without a job, homeless, and separated from my husband all in the same week. I was in denial. I couldn't believe any of this was happening. You see, I had known him since I was five years old. Our families were friends. I had loved him all my life and married him because I believed he would never hurt me, but now, here I was—hurt.

I had never asked God if he was the right man to marry. Honestly, I can't remember thinking about it for more than a minute before I said yes. A few people urged me not to do it. I wanted the dream, the marriage, the house, and the children. I moved to Florida, didn't pray about it, and a year later we were married. We had our challenges, but I did not imagine that four years later I would be getting divorced. Relationships can be challenging; however, if you are both focused on your relationship with God when obstacles arise, you can work on them together. When one person does not have the same belief system as you, it is difficult to resolve those issues.

After this heartbreak, I stayed in Florida, hoping he would reconsider working on the relationship. When he didn't, two years later, I moved back to New York. I was destructive. I hated that I was back home, divorced, with no children. It was only then, when I had nowhere else to turn, that I began attending church again. I had not been to church in over ten years. I had finally begun looking for healing. I attended a divorce support group at church, but I still did not have a relationship with the Lord. I began dating, but I didn't care if the man had a girlfriend, wife, or whatever his situation was if he was giving me attention. I was in pain. I still had limiting beliefs. I did not think that anyone would ever love me.

Then I found someone who I could see myself with. We went to church together, volunteered in the community, and enjoyed each other's company. But I was not healed, so I broke it off. When I tried to make amends, he called me a liar. I was so offended; I had never lied to him. However, he disagreed. He told me that I lied every time I wasn't true to myself. Every time I did something to please him that I didn't want to do. He was right. You cannot love anyone until you love yourself. Limiting beliefs are healed when you learn that God loves you just as you are.

It was time to activate my faith, to let go of the past, but I kept asking myself, how did I not see that my marriage was in trouble? Am I not worthy of anyone loving me? Why won't he fight for me and our marriage? Why don't my relationships last? These questions led me to understand that I lacked faith in the Lord. Do you lack faith? Do you trust Him with all your heart? It seemed like all the women who were trying to support me through this difficult time in my life had unwavering faith. I deeply respected these women and wanted to be radiant like they were. If you want that in your life, it is time to be dauntless in obtaining it.

Something in my life had to change. I had to make bold moves to drastically improve my life. I started going to a Christian Cultural Center where they pride themselves on being a teaching church, where the congregation doesn't just listen to the word, but studies it. I started to learn. I started to believe. My spirit was filled with God's love. The holy spirit spoke to me while I was there. I cried. I found myself.

It is imperative that you act. I started by letting go of a lot of people who I had considered friends at the time. It was extremely hard to do at first, but evaluating the people in your life who do not add value and instead drain your life, is healthy for your spirit. It was necessary because once I got to know myself intimately, I realized I had not created proper boundaries with them.

I started to go to Bible study religiously. I was there every Tuesday, eager to learn. I joined the singles ministry at my church to figure out what I had done wrong—why I kept attracting men who would leave me. This began my healing process. For the first time in my life, I was getting to know God. Trusting God is also about trusting yourself and trusting your spirit. "For he says, 'In the time of favor I heard you, and in the day of salvation I helped you.' I tell you, now is the time of God's favor, now is the day of salvation" (2 Corinthians 6:2 NIV).

To continue to grow in my faith, I had to continue to act. The following actions can help you reestablish a relationship with the Lord:

- Seek the Lord first for everything.

- Declare your life to God.

- Attend church regularly.

- Take notes in church.

- Keep a journal.

- Join a Bible study.

- Go to spiritual counseling.

- Find a divinity or spiritual coach.

- Become an active member in a ministry.

- Create a prayer circle with your family and friends.

Find what works for you. It could be something from my list or something completely different. Ask God to help you find the best choice for your personal healing.

I had additional support from my best friend, Cynthia, my sorority sister, Erika, and my sister-in-law, Janey. Don't be scared to look and ask for help from the people in your life who have always been there for you. My best friend had been through a divorce and was instrumental in helping me deal with my emotions. She always reminded me of my strengths, and I will always love her for that. I saw Erika's journey with the Lord, and she became a role model for me. She also recommended I go to therapy. I learned to talk to God about my problems, and I learned that everything is a lesson for my growth and to cast all my worries on the Lord. Janey kept my spirits up. She kept me motivated and looking at next steps. Her strength pulled me like a magnet. She was my rock. Find someone you trust. Listen to them. Allow them to be blessings in your life.

There were several issues that led to my divorce. One of them was my inability to bear his child. I have polycystic ovarian syndrome, making it difficult to conceive. While married, we unsuccessfully tried to conceive with infertility treatments.

After my divorce, I thought I would never be a mom. How could I have ever doubted God? In 2013, my big blessing was manifested when I received a phone call to be the foster parent to my newborn niece and daughter, Elizabeth. She is the best thing that has ever happened to me. I kept saying, Lord, you got jokes! Ha! My Father, the King always shows me how much He loves me. He will show you too!

Do you trust the Lord? Do you go to Him first with all your worries? Are your desires in alignment with what God wants for your life? "Set your minds on what is above, not on what is on earth" (Colossians 3:2 CSB). I want to encourage you to remember to fully trust in God's plan for your life. Having faith can be challenging at times, but He will not desert you. He knows what is in your heart, but most of all what is best for you. Walk with faith and have joy in your heart. The solution to every challenge in your life is, "Do not be afraid or discouraged. For the Lord your God is with you wherever you go" (Joshua 1:9 NLT).

Your Road Has a Purpose

Evelina C. Smith

Have you ever traveled down the road you thought you knew the end to, only to find out there's a detour? This road had curves, turn offs, yields, and hills, so as a divorced, single mother who raised two sons, I had to do whatever it took during this detour to keep a sound mind and provide for my two sons. The detour was my divorce, which can take you on a long or roundabout route of several obstacles, but slowly and surely, God put me back on my path. It's amazing how God redeems the time!

As little girls, we are taught to grow up and get married and live happily ever after, so at the age of twenty-five, I moved from Maryland to New Jersey, landed a great job in a law firm on Fifth Avenue in New York, got married, had two handsome sons, and lived the married life for eleven years—until the relationship took a turn for the worse and ended in divorce. I had no family other than my church family in New Jersey, so I was surrounded by people of faith, which is so important when trying to deal with a situation alone. My church brothers and sisters supported and prayed for us.

I grew up in church, and though my parents were married, it was really my mother who raised me and taught me to always try and never give up because things would get better. She showed me how to have joy and exercise my faith during times of lack. I still laugh today because I thought it was a treat to have breakfast for dinner, when in actuality, it was an inexpensive, easy, and filling meal for that evening and something that was common in our culture. So with good memories like that, I have been determined to raise God-fearing sons and to keep a sound mind. My faith has always kept me knowing that I know where my help comes from. The strength I have has been built through prayer and has kept us striving. I asked God every night to provide for our needs and He did just that by this simple prayer: Dear Spirit of the true living God, I ask that You take care of me and my sons. "And my God shall supply all your need according to His riches in glory by Christ Jesus" (Philippians 4:19 NKJV).

I had a few defining moments in my life when I wanted more after divorce and more after my second son graduated from high school. I wanted to take responsibility for my life and to have more to my eulogy than "She was a good mother." I wanted to be a positive influence for people and know that I had enjoyed my life and was real. I wanted to encourage, inspire, and have a purpose to help people get where they needed to be. I knew I was the only person to change my mindset about my circumstances. However, in order to change my circumstances, I first had to confront the key issues that were interrupting my life, such as feeling stressed, feeling inadequate, missing opportunities, thinking I didn't know the right people, and never having enough finances.

I used to ask myself, why am I not doing something to change my circumstances? Why is everyone else around me prospering? Why am I expecting things to change doing the same thing? Why haven't I given myself permission to change to get from hiding in the back to sitting in the front, going from being quiet to being outspoken, from being uneducated to being educated, and from being small to being big? But then, as I kept studying God's word, I realized I represent the kingdom. I'm an example. I'm being ministered to by good people and am realizing that they are no different than I am; they serve the same God I do and He is no respecter of persons. So it let me see that people are constantly moving and doing something—and whether through big leaps or small leaps, it's motion. And so, this passage inspired me: "Brethen, I do not count myself to have apprehended; but one thing I do, forgetting those things which are behind and reaching forward to those things which are ahead, I press toward the goal for the prize of the upward call of God in Christ Jesus" (Philippians 3:13-14 NKJV). It made me take that leap. I took a moment in time and said, "All right, I'm going to do this. I'm not going to focus on what I don't have or my past mistakes. I'm going to do something new. I'm going to do something I've never done before." And I did it! I moved.

I finally got tired of only doing predictable activities and what was expected of me—for instance, coming and going to work and church, picking up and dropping off my sons from their extracurricular activities, and socializing with the same people. So as a single mom, I took a bold step. I trusted God's word with a feeling of assurance from this passage: "The steps of a good man are ordered by the Lord, And He delights in his way.

Though he fall, he shall not be utterly cast down; For the Lord upholds him with His hand" (Psalm 37:23-24 NKJV). I stepped out and walked by faith and began to build my business. It was essential because I not only needed extra income every month, but I wanted to leave a legacy for my sons. I needed to discover more of me and who I was and what I was made of. That being said, I'm a person that inspires and motivates others to do better or at least try and see the direction of the outcome. You can go into a situation one way and come out another way with great results. People look at me and realize that if I can do it, they can do it too. I have learned that I am made with tons of courage. I do many things not knowing how to do it or not having a full picture of its outcome, but I'll do it anyway. I'll do it afraid but confident that the outcome will turn out for my good.

During the transformation and building of my business, I learned to trust God and not man because man will fail you. I had to remember that everyone does not support my vision and may not be happy for me. I first had to invest in myself, so God led me to resources and people who have mastered and do well in business. As I grow in business, I read more and attend events that promote self-development, which is fun because I have been able to travel all over the country. I get a chance to mix business with pleasure.

As I have sowed into myself, God has watered and shined on everything I have put my hands into. There were times when I grew weary in well-doing, but God still provided. I had to learn that God is still good even when I endured hardships, betrayals, and temptations. Those were the times I grew more in Him. I learned lessons to live now and plan and set goals for my future.

There was a time all I thought about were plans for my future because my now was so overwhelming. It's nice to plan the future; you need to know where you are going, but throughout life, situations can deter your plans for the future. So I live for now while I have the energy to go and continue to develop. I have more time for myself, and there are things that I just need to do now that will serve its purpose for my future.

There are times when God will tell you to move now. I had to let go of the mistakes and pain of my past because there was nothing I could change about that. I learned to stop concerning myself with standards of what other people felt I should do and instead do what I'm interested in doing. I also learned that I have to be more active in church and outside of church so I can encourage a broken or hopeless soul and love and care for them the way Christ has for me.

If I were in the same situation today, I would ask myself questions like, what comes naturally to me? What do I love to do? What routine have I created that needs to be broken because it adds no value to my life? Whom do I find consistency and comfort in? Whom do I know that is growing and successful in business? Whom do I know that is genuine, transparent, and down to earth that I can learn from? What am I afraid of? How determined am I to want out of a certain situation? Can I still manage and maintain my priorities while I'm transitioning into the change? How much time can I put into it? What is my "why" for change? These questions are vital because they helped me learn a lesson on how much time I could save and what direction I was going in. People generally respond and walk with a confidence when they know where they are going. The most valuable thing I have is my time and not my possessions. I have learned I cannot get back time, so I use it wisely.

If you are going through the same situation I went through, pray all your concerns to God, never isolate yourself, and share your concerns, fears, and dreams with positive people who are progressing and doing something that you may want to do. The very reason I say that is because people connect people, so you don't know who you will meet who will help take you to where you are going. I would also say to you to make up your mind to go forward and never accept being comfortable hanging back. Don't give up when running into challenges, and let people know you are stuck.

My big blessing has manifested yet it is still evolving. I think back on how I didn't know how I was going to raise my sons or what was going to become of them without having their father in their lives. Yet, today, they are both in college doing well, working, very articulate, very intelligent, God-fearing young men. I am able to give sound advice on how to trust God's instructions and know that prayer works. I am now confident in how I connect and network with progressing resources and people because I have learned to ask for help and I know who I am. My needs are provided for, and I don't struggle at the end of every month in search of a handout or child support. I am able to lead and share tips on business because I am an entrepreneur with a thriving, healthy business that helps people financially and physically. I am standing strong today giving honor to God for navigating me through my detour. The road had curves, turn offs, yields, and hills, and I went on a long or roundabout route, but I'm wiser and back on the road to my destination.

"Success is liking yourself, liking what you do, and liking how you do it."

—Maya Angelou

"When you learn, teach. When you get, give."
—Maya Angelou

About the Authors

RANELLI WILLIAMS

Ranelli Williams is a certified public accountant, bestselling author, speaker, entrepreneur, and legacy building catalyst who works with faith-based entrepreneurs and couples to master their money as they work toward building a strong financial legacy. With her husband, Eric Williams, Ranelli is the cofounder of ERJ Services, LLC, a tax and accounting solutions business that provides services to individuals, small businesses, and nonprofits. Ranelli is also the cofounder of the L.I.F.T. Conference, which serves faith-based women in business and ministry.

After graduating from Borough of Manhattan Community College with an associate's degree in business management, she went on to earn her bachelor's degree in accounting and a master of business administration (MBA) at Baruch College. She is currently pursuing a doctor of business administration (DBA) in entrepreneurship at Walden University.

As author of the book, *Releasing the Fear and Walking in Faith,* she brings to life the blessings, miracles, and life-changing manifestations that occur in peoples' lives when they fully put their trust in God. Ranelli and her husband live in East Stroudsburg, Pennsylvania, with their sons, Joeraan and Jaevaan.

To connect, visit her website at www.ranelliwilliams.com

ALLISON DENISE ARNETT

Allison Denise, the builder of Beautiful Brands and a Be-You-Tiful You, is known as the Creative Accountant because of her twenty years of experience in accounting and thirteen years of experience in graphic and web design. In the past year, she has helped over seventy speakers, authors, and coaches make their brands more beautiful, marketable, and profitable with services such as web design, speaker one-sheets, book covers, logos, and more.

When she is not building beautiful brands, Allison can be found in her hometown of Houston, Texas, advocating self-acceptance and loving on her three beautiful babies.

To learn more about her services and courses, go to www.ImAllisonDenise.com

DELMAR JOHNSON

With over twenty years of experience working with big corporations, small business owners, and new entrepreneurs, human resource guru and visionary Delmar Johnson founded HR Brain for Hire™ as a trusted and resourceful solution for first-time employers in need of affordable, efficient, and top-notch recruitment, training, and HR solutions. Delmar's personal story, which includes multiple layoffs, challenges, and her own dive into entrepreneurship, gives her a perfect mix of formal knowledge and real-life experience that she pours into each client and their unique needs. Business owners love Delmar, as her talent and passion for HR allow them to fall in love with their business all over again.

Delmar is an award-nominated author of *Seasons of My Soul: A Life Journey Through Lessons Learned in a Dry Place*, and an award-nominated entrepreneur who's been featured in *The Working Mother* and *Connected Woman* magazines.

Learn more at www.delmarjohnson.com

DR. CHERYLANN JORDAN, ND

Dr. Cherylann Jordan, ND, is a wellness coach for women over forty, lifestyle strategist, and naturopath doctor with a background in civil engineering and construction. While a stay-at-home mom, Dr. Jordan completed her degree in health and wellness and graduated as an ND.

As an author, speaker, wellness coach, medical missionary, and creator of the Rejuvenate Your Life Blueprint, she has mentored and coached women, specifically over the age of forty, to successfully lose weight and change their lifestyle so that they can have incredible health.

A native of the island of Trinidad, Dr. Jordan currently resides in Effort, Pennsylvania. She is a devoted wife of thirty-two years to her husband, Stephen, and mother of four adult children. She has ten grandchildren and one great-grandson.

To learn more, visit her website at Cherylannjordan.com

NATAUSHIA MILLER

Nataushia Miller is an ambassador for Christ, wife, mother, author, speaker, and visionary. She began her human service career while in high school, as a caretaker for children with physical and mental disabilities, before she obtained her BA in sociology and social welfare from Dillard University of New Orleans in 2006. Later, she received her MA in community leadership from the American Baptist Seminary of the West of Berkeley in 2011.

Nataushia Miller is a Toastmasters Competent Speaker and FREEDOM Coach with a mission to help you reach higher levels of freedom in your life. Her motto is "FREEDOM is who you are and can create." She is the CEO of Character 4 Life Global and cofounder and publishing consultant of Stagecraft Publishing. Nataushia enjoys reading, dancing, traveling, meeting new people, and living life with her husband Andre and three children: Keturah, Audrey Abigail, and Jonas Miller.

To learn more about Nataushia Miller and her Freedom movement, go to www.c4lglobal.com

VERONICA RAY

Veronica Ray is the founder and chief number cruncher at Jigsaw & Associates. She attributes her success to faith in God and loves every minute of this divinely orchestrated adventure. With her amazing ability to connect with people, Veronica goes beyond the numbers and contributes real-world value through meaningful relationships and professional services.

Her belief that real results come from understanding you—the business owner—and not just your business feeds her personal mission to help entrepreneurs succeed in business and build financially solid companies. Veronica's training tool box includes a wealth of information chosen specifically to help you obtain your goals and sustain growing profit margins.

In her free time, Veronica loves to spend time with her children and granddaughter. She also serves as a board member for a local nonprofit organization and generously donates her time to other local companies.

To learn more about Veronica Ray, and her business, please visit www.jigsaw-associates.com

DR. WILLIAM IRISH-O'BRIEN

Dr. William Irish-O'Brien currently holds the position as director of nursing at a long-term care facility in the New York area for the past three years. He has earned a BSBA, MBA, and a DM from the University of Phoenix. Dr. Irish-O'Brien has the distinction of becoming the first registered male nurse in the history of Montserrat, the Caribbean island of his birth. He has been recognized for his contribution and achievements by the Montserrat Progressive Society in New York.

Dr. O'Brien has worked extensively in long-term care as director of nursing. A motivational speaker, teacher, actor, and singer, he has conducted health seminars, assisted with planning and executing health fairs, and worked as a youth director within the church.

Dr. Irish-O'Brien enjoys writing and is laying the groundwork for the release of his first book. He currently lives in Orange New Jersey.

To connect with Dr. Irish-O'Brien, email corkhill989@gmail.com

Dr. Bernice Bramble

Dr. Bernice Bramble, a registered nurse born in Montserrat, has over forty-five years of healthcare experience and currently works as a patient care coordinator in New York City. She holds a bachelor of science in nursing from Lehman College, a dual master in business administration and community health from Long Island University, and a PhD in human services from Capella University.

Dr. Bramble is member of the New York State Nurses Association, the American Association of Critical Care Nurses, and the Association of Wound Care Nurses, and a lifetime member of the Worldwide Association of Notable Alumni. Author of *The Study of Family Life Education in Montserrat* and *The Lived Experience of Senior Nurses Working with Health Information Technology in their Daily Practice*, Dr. Bramble is a life-long learner who likes to serve by mentoring and training nurses and living her life with humility and grace.

To contact her, email Babramble@yahoo.com

DR. GARRETT INGRAM

Dr. Garrett Ingram is a visionary, consultant, therapist, and holistic coach focused on helping individuals overcome adversities. As the founder of Upward & Onward Messages and Object Lessons, with a blog on Facebook and Word Press, he provides holistic coaching and consultation designed to strengthen family dynamics and help families overcome adversities.

Dr. Ingram currently serves as an Elder at Mount Pocono Temple of Seven Day Adventist as well as the Men Ministry Leader and Family Life Leader. Dr. Ingram is motivated to help individuals unlock their God-given potential by igniting their resilient processes and guiding them in experiencing healthy transformational experiences, to becoming change agents, and to sharing their experiences with others to help them overcome adversities too.

To connect with Dr. Ingram, email him at Drgingram@gmail.com

DR. SYLVIA E. EPHRAIM

Dr. Sylvia E. Ephraim holds a faculty position in higher education, teaching both graduate and undergraduate students at King Graduate School of Business and Berkeley College.

Dr. Ephraim graduated with distinction after earning a post master's certificate in education and a doctor of philosophy in organization and management, publishing her dissertation in 2014. A member of the Business Honor Society Sigma Beta Delta, she was the first recipient of the David M. Gordon Memorial Award for outstanding work in economics from Bronx Community College.

A strong believer that she can do all things through Christ, and it is her faith that has brought her thus far, she knows her journey can be a reality for anyone who believes.

To contact Dr. Ephraim, email her at sephraim35@gmail.com

Victor T. Olufemi

Victor T. Olufemi is a chartered accountant of the Institute of Chartered Accountants of Nigeria (ICAN). He is versed in financial and accounts management and business planning, and experienced with systems and process documentation for review and improvement. Victor is information technology savvy and enriches his versatility with research and continued learning. Having earned a master of business administration from Obafemi Awolowo University, Ile-Ife, Nigeria, he is currently at the concluding stage, earning a doctor of business administration (DBA) at Walden University in the United States.

As a lover of music and outside academics, Victor is the director of music at his local church assembly.

To connect, email him at vicot1201@yahoo.com

Elizabeth Lindsey

Elizabeth Lindsey has been a registered nurse for over forty years, of which twenty were spent giving service in her native island of the West Indies where she worked as a nurse anesthetist, midwife, and staff nurse before immigrating to the United States. Presently, she is working in the Infection Control Department as an assistant nursing director/infection preventionist.

Prior to this assignment, she worked in critical care areas, specialty clinics, and occupational health services as head nurse/clinical instructor, assistant head nurse, staff nurse, and graduate nurse. She also worked as per diem supervisor in long-term care facilities and adjunct professor at private and community colleges. A trained legal nurse consultant and PRI assessor, Elizabeth obtained her bachelor's degree in nursing from Herbert H. Lehman Community College and a master's degree in healthcare administration from Bellevue University, and she is currently pursuing her doctor of nursing practice.

To connect with Elizabeth Lindsey, email salworth1@ gmail.com

La'Shonda DeBrew

La'Shonda DeBrew is the founder of the Wealthcheck 360 Institute and the Wealthcheck 360 System™. She is a seasoned and savvy entrepreneur, tax strategist, retirement specialist, speaker, and one of the nation's leading authorities in the areas of tax planning, debt destruction, and financial strategy.

In addition to her ability to stay in action, get results, manage successful outcomes, and be innovative, she shows clients how to increase and grow their bottom line daily. La'Shonda's passion and proficiency is in saving clients time, money, and energy, so that they can make more, keep more, give more, and ultimately live more. With the motto, "If you can perceive it, believe it, you can achieve it," she works with driven, excuse-free womenpreneurs who struggle with finding financial peace to help them live in financial freedom and establish their path to wealth.

To connect, visit www.lashondadebrew.com

KIM JONES

Kim Jones is a professional motivational speaker, certified personal life coach, career strategist, and author with the vision to assist women in reaching their true potential and create transformation through the setting of self-defined goals. Kim has an extensive background in the area of corporate training, coaching, and personal development. Working in the capacity of a trainer and coach has evolved her into a skilled facilitator with the ability to connect with and inspire any audience. Her teaching and facilitating style propels people to take action for optimal success, as she interacts with her audience and allows them to break down the barriers. As a trusted go-to source for expert guidance, Kim inspires women to stand up, step into their destiny, and redesign their life's blueprint.

To learn more about Kim Jones, visit www.kimjonespeaking.com

DEE EDWARDS

Master business coach, speaker, and author, Dee Edwards dedicates her time working with new and aspiring entrepreneurs and business owners to help build profitable and sustainable startup businesses. As the CEO of The Startup Business Factory, she provides training, coaching, accountability, and support as well as a host of other individualized services to help move startup business owners from frustration to execution. As a result of working with her, small business owners are equipped with the tools, knowledge, training, resources, and accountability to think bigger as an entrepreneur, reach higher in their business goals, and generate continuous profits.

To connect with Dee Edwards, visit www.DeeEdwardsOnline.com

CHEZLINE RILEY

A native of Montserrat, West Indies, Chezline Riley immigrated to the United States when she was fourteen and went on to earn a bachelor of business administration in human resources management from Baruch College, City University of New York, in 1999. Until 2010, she worked in higher education as a financial aid professional and then returned to her home country, teaching business, accounting, and ICT, and serving as head of the business/IT department. Currently, Chezline resides in London, United Kingdom, as a contract administrator in the strategic property services division within the London Borough of Hackney. A devoted Christian and educator by nature, she is passionate about youth ministry and music, and dedicates her time and resources to guiding young people toward achieving their full potential.

To connect, email her at Riley.Chezline@gmail.com

MARCELLA D. MOORE

Marcella D. Moore, affectionately known as "Cella D" is an inspirational speaker, motivator, mentor, and author. She is the founder of the weekly Motivate and Pray empowerment call and the monthly Caring for the Caregiver support call, both of which serve as a resource for motivation, inspiration, empowerment, and prayer.

Marcella is the coauthor of the Amazon bestselling book *Tainted Elegance: Simply Beautiful*, a work that gives young women the courage to say "I love who I am." Her professional career includes more than thirty years in the corporate world as manager, director, and account executive. Marcella's life journey has birthed a message in her that says, "Be a part of your own rescue, embrace your journey, live on purpose, and love yourself to life." Cella D's prayer is that the light of God on her life shines bright enough to make hearts open, babies leap, and sleeping giants awake.

Learn more at www.marcelladmoore.com

STEPHNIE A. GREGORY

Stephnie A. Gregory was born in Antigua and Barbuda. She is an administrator, business owner, mentor, and motivator, as well as an independent certified coach, teacher, and speaker with the John Maxwell Team. She holds a degree in business administration and organizational management, with a major in human resources and a minor in marketing. An active member of Lambda Kappa Mu Sorority, Inc., or LKM, Stephnie is a network marketer, DSWA-certified leader who trains and mentors teams around the United States to become successful business owners. She was recently awarded the Spirit of Albee Award in recognition for dedication, service, and sales leadership. With her motto of "stay focused," she believes that nothing is impossible. The sky is the limit once you reposition yourself to soar.

Learn more at www.stephniegregory.com

ANGELA PIZARRO

A native New Yorker who has made her home in Pennsylvania with her family, Angela Pizarro has a passion for encouraging others through her candid experiences and undiscovered strength through life's disappointments and triumphs.

Angela credits her main lessons in life to living a life of obedience and final surrendering to God. Her education came in the way of helping others, as her door remains open for all who need guidance counseling and love. Her story will encourage you to never frown at small beginnings wherever you find yourself in life. Her jewelry company, TreClara, offers unique, handcrafted designs. No two pieces are exactly alike. There is something for everyone!

For more information, contact her at Gap4ever2@gmail.com

KHALIMA GREEN

Khalima Green is the marketing director of Mountaintop Retreat and Conference Center. Previously, she upheld corporate professional positions in the health insurance industry for many years. She is currently working on her AAS in business management from Northampton Community College. Originating from New York, Khalima is currently residing in Pennsylvania with her two children.

For more information please email her at Khalima.green@gmail.com

OHILDA HOLGUIN

Personal development expert Ohilda Holguin is COO of Elite Consulting Group, co-owner of Sistah Chat Global Media, and founder of a women's online empowerment platform. Called the "Self-Discovery Coach," she is an author, speaker, radio personality, and life coach.

Ohilda holds a bachelor of psychology and business, and a master of education. She is a master Reiki practitioner, an emotional freedom techniques facilitator, and is currently being certified as an Ayurveda health counselor. She has received an Award for Excellence in Community Action, and a Monroe County Image Award with the cohosts of Sistah Chat Radio Show. Her mission establishes a global platform to help women listen to their spirit, connect to energy, speak their truth, and heal unconscious limiting patterns of beliefs that hold her back from success in life and business.

Learn more about Ohilda Holguin at www.Ohilda.com

EVELINA SMITH

Evelina Smith is an entrepreneur and CEO and founder of Beanbliss, a healthy living home-based business. In addition, she is certified by the American Bar Association (ABA) as a patent paralegal.

A single mom, Evelina understands the day-to-day challenges of building a successful business and raising a family in today's competitive marketplace. She has a focused business sense that has resulted in her achieving numerous accolades as a home-based business leader.

Evelina keeps a positive spirit, does not give up easily, and works around her obstacles to achieve her dreams. She will help you leverage your time and resources to create a business around your passion, dreams, and lifestyle. Her purpose and mission is to encourage and inspire single women to excel and live outside the box of what could seem impossible with less.

Learn more by contacting her at beanbliss2014@gmail.com

Sources

Unless otherwise indicated, scripture quotations are from the Holy Bible, King James Version. All rights reserved.

Scriptures marked NIV are taken from the New International Version®. Copyright © 1973, 1978, 1984, 2011 by Biblica, Inc.™. All rights reserved.

Scriptures marked NLT are taken from the New Living Translation®. Copyright © 1996, 2004, 2007, 2013 by Tyndale House Foundation. All rights reserved.

Scriptures marked BSB are taken from The Holy Bible, Berean Study Bible, BSB Copyright ©2016 by Bible Hub. Used by Permission. All Rights Reserved Worldwide.

Scriptures marked ESV are taken from English Standard Version®. Copyright © 2001 by Crossway, a publishing ministry of Good News Publishers. All rights reserved.

Scriptures marked ISV are taken from *The Holy Bible: International Standard Version*. Release 2.0, Build 2015.02.09. Copyright © 1995-2014 by ISV Foundation. ALL RIGHTS RESERVED INTERNATIONALLY. Used by permission of Davidson Press, LLC.

Scriptures marked CSB are taken from The Christian Standard Bible. Copyright © 2017 by Holman Bible Publishers. Used by permission. Christian Standard Bible®, and CSB® are federally registered trademarks of Holman Bible Publishers, all rights reserved.

CREATING DISTINCTIVE BOOKS
WITH INTENTIONAL RESULTS

We're a collaborative group of creative masterminds
with a mission to produce high-quality books to position
you for monumental success in the marketplace.

Our professional team of writers, editors, designers,
and marketing strategists work closely together to ensure
that every detail of your book is a clear representation
of the message in your writing.

Want to know more?

Write to us at info@publishyourgift.com
or call (888) 949-6228

Discover great books, exclusive offers, and more at
www.PublishYourGift.com

Connect with us on social media

@publishyourgift

www.ingramcontent.com/pod-product-compliance
Lightning Source LLC
Chambersburg PA
CBHW071727160225

22014CB00041B/529

9 781947 054066